SABBATH AS RESISTANCE
NEW EDITION WITH STUDY GUIDE

Also by Walter Brueggemann
from Westminster John Knox Press

Abiding Astonishment: Psalms, Modernity, and the Making of History
    (Literary Currents in Biblical Interpretation series)
Cadences of Hope: Preaching among Exiles
Celebrating Abundance: Devotions for Advent
Chosen? Reading the Bible amid the Israeli-Palestinian Conflict
The Collected Sermons of Walter Brueggemann, Volumes 1 and 2
First and Second Samuel (Interpretation series)
From Whom No Secrets Are Hid: Introducing the Psalms
Genesis (Interpretation series)
Gift and Task: A Year of Daily Readings and Reflections
Great Prayers of the Old Testament
Hope for the World: Mission in a Global Context
Hope within History
*An Introduction to the Old Testament: The Canon and Christian
    Imagination, Second Edition* (with Tod A. Linafelt)
Isaiah 1–39 (Westminster Bible Companion series)
Isaiah 40–66 (Westminster Bible Companion series)
Journey to the Common Good
Living Countertestimony: Conversations with Walter Brueggemann (with
    Carolyn J. Sharp)
Mandate to Difference: An Invitation to the Contemporary Church
Many Voices, One God: Being Faithful in a Pluralistic World (with
    George W. Stroup)
Power, Providence, and Personality: Bibilcal Insight into Life and Ministry
*Reverberations of Faith: A Theological Handbook of Old Testament
    Themes*
Struggling with Scripture (with Brian K. Blount and William C.
    Placher)
Texts for Preaching: A Lectionary Commentary (with Charles B.
    Cousar, Beverly Roberts Gaventa, J. Clinton McCann, and
    James D. Newsome)
Truth Speaks to Power: The Countercultural Nature of Scripture
Using God's Resources Wisely: Isaiah and Urban Possibility
The Vitality of Old Testament Traditions, Second Edition (with Hans
    Walter Wolff)
A Way other than Our Own: Devotions for Lent (compiled by Richard
    Floyd)

SABBATH AS RESISTANCE
NEW EDITION
WITH STUDY GUIDE

Saying No to the Culture of Now

WALTER BRUEGGEMANN

WJK WESTMINSTER
JOHN KNOX PRESS
LOUISVILLE · KENTUCKY

Portions of this book were previously published as a downloadable study titled "Sabbath as Resistance," The Thoughtful Christian, August 1, 2007, www.TheThoughtfulChristian.com.

Revised edition
Published by Westminster John Knox Press
Louisville, Kentucky

17 18 19 20 21 22 23 24 25 26—10 9 8 7 6 5 4 3 2 1

Book design by Erika Lundbom-Krift
Cover design by Dilu Nicholas

Library of Congress Cataloging-in-Publication Data

Names: Brueggemann, Walter, author.
Title: Sabbath as resistance : saying no to the culture of now / Walter Brueggemann.
Description: New Edition, with Study Guide. | Louisville, KY : Westminster John Knox Press, 2017. |
Identifiers: LCCN 2017029410 (print) | LCCN 2017032186 (ebook) | ISBN 9781611648300 (ebk.) | ISBN 9780664263294 (pbk. : alk. paper)
Subjects: LCSH: Sabbath. | Sunday. | Rest--Religious aspects--Christianity.
Classification: LCC BV111.3 (ebook) | LCC BV111.3 .B77 2017 (print) | DDC 296.4/1--dc23
LC record available at https://lccn.loc.gov/2017029410

Most Westminster John Knox Press books are available at special quantity discounts when purchased in bulk by corporations, organizations, and special-interest groups. For more information, please e-mail SpecialSales @wjkbooks.com.

*In memory of my mother, Hilda,
and Charles,
the son she loved first*

CONTENTS

PREFACE

FOR THE MOST PART, CONTEMPORARY CHRISTIANS PAY LITTLE attention to the Sabbath. We more or less know that the day came to reflect, in U.S. culture, the most stringent disciplinary faith of the Puritans which, in recent time, translated into a moralistic prescription for a day of quiet restraint and prohibition. In many, somewhat-pietistic homes that amounted to not playing cards or seeing films on Sunday, and certainly not shopping. I can remember each year debates in our rural community about farmers working on some few Sundays to harvest wheat in the face of devastating rains that were sure to come. I can remember from my earlier days, moreover, that because of "Blue Laws," Sunday home baseball games for the Phillies and the Pirates in Pennsylvania could not begin a new inning after 6:00

p.m. The sum of all these memories of restraint was essentially negative, a series of "Thou Shalt Nots" that served to echo the more fundamental prohibitions of the Decalogue. This context did not offer much potential for seeing the Sabbath in a positive way as an affirmative declaration of faith or identity. And, of course, as church monopoly in our culture has in many places waned or disappeared, the commitment to Sabbath discipline has likewise receded.

As in so many things concerning Christian faith and practice, we have to be reeducated by Judaism that has been able to sustain its commitment to Sabbath as a positive practice of faith.[1] The magisterial book of Abraham Heschel continues to be a lead voice in a Jewish awareness of Sabbath.[2] In our present context, perhaps it is Michael Fishbane's eloquent probe of Jewish practices that has the most to teach us about Jewish understandings of Sabbath.[3] Fishbane's discussion is in the larger context of his splendid book concerning the maintenance of Jewish "mindfulness" in a society that is increasingly "mindless." The Sabbath, along with the other practices he exposits, concerns the maintenance of a distinct faith identity in the midst of a culture that is inhospitable to all distinct identities in its impatient reduction of all human life to the requirements of the market. In contrast (and contradiction) to cultural mindlessness (that can hardly be underestimated!):

> The Sabbath and its observance may cultivate a theological mindfulness. . . .
>
> How so?
>
> The Sabbath sanctifies time through sanctioned forms of rest and inaction. On this day certain work-

aday activities and ordinary busyness are suspended
and brought to a halt. In their stead, a whole host
of ways of resting the body and mind are cultivated.
These are of a special cultural type. For though we
have a natural notion of work, and think of it in
terms of physical exertion or compulsory performance done in order to sustain one's livelihood,
these kinds of labor relate to our Adamic selves: the
physical self that is sent forth into the world and
must work the earth to provide sustenance, while
losing body strength on one's life-course toward
death. By contrast, our Mosaic selves are enhanced
through the teachings of the Oral Torah, which
bring other notions of work and categories of labor
to bear.[4]

Fishbane contrasts the "Adamic self," the one of natural creatureliness, with the "Mosaic self" that comes
under the sway of the Mosaic commands of Sinai. The
Sabbath is a sphere of inaction.

One enters the sphere of inaction through divestment,
and this release affects all the elements of the worka-
day sphere. Business activity and exchange of money
are forbidden, and one is urged not just to desist from
commerce but to develop more interior spheres of set-
tling the mind from this type of agitation. . . . Slowly,
under these multiple conditions, a sense of inaction
takes over, and the day does not merely mark the
stoppage of work or celebrate the completion of creation, but enforces the value that the earth is a gift of
divine creativity, given to humankind in sacred trust.
On the Sabbath, the practical benefits of technology
are laid aside, and one tries to stand in the cycle of
natural time, without manipulation or interference.
To the degree possible, one must attempt to bring the
qualities of inaction and rest into the heart and mind.
. . . The Sabbath is thus a period of sacred stasis, a

duration of sanctity through the cultivation of inaction in body and spirit. . . .

The heartbeat of repose may thus suffuse the mind and limbs of one's being, and generate an inner balance poised on quietude and a settled spirit.[5]

The choice of an economic image by Fishbane, "divestment," suggests that we may consider the sabbath as an alternative to the endless demands of economic reality, more specifically the demands of market ideology that depend, as Adam Smith had already seen, on the generation of needs and desires that will leave us endlessly "rest-less," inadequate, unfulfilled, and in pursuit of that which may satiate desire. Those requirements concern endless predation so that we are a society of 24/7 multitasking in order to achieve, accomplish, perform, and possess. But the demands of market ideology pertain as much to consumption as they do to production. Thus the system of commodity requires that we want more, have more, own more, use more, eat more, and drink more. The rat race of such predation and usurpation is a restlessness that issues inescapably in anxiety that is often at the edge of being unmanageable; when pursued vigorously enough, moreover, one is propelled to violence against the neighbor in eagerness for what properly belongs to the neighbor.

As acute as this is for us in our society, this is not an unprecedented or even new situation. It is, as Judaism remembers, as old as Pharaoh's insatiable script for production. It is impossible to imagine that in the system of Pharaoh there could ever be any restfulness for anyone (see Exod. 5:4–19). Most remarkably Israel, in the narrative, finally is delivered from Pharaoh's anxiety system and comes to the wilderness; there Israel is given bread that it is not permitted to store up (Exod. 16:13–21). But even more remarkable, even in such a marginal context, with daily need for bread that is given for the day, provision is made for the Sabbath. Israel cannot store up bread for more than a day; except (big "except"!) on the sixth day Israel may store up enough for the seventh day so that it can rest on that day (vv. 22–24). This unexpected provision is surely a sign that this bread for life is not under the demanding governance of Pharaoh; it is under the sustaining rule of the creator God. Even in the wilderness with scarce resources, God mandates a pause for Sabbath for the community:

> Eat it today, for today is a sabbath to the LORD; today you will not find it in the field. Six days you shall gather it, but on the seventh day, which is a sabbath, there will be none.
>
> On the seventh day some of the people went out to gather, and they found none. The LORD said to Moses, "How long will you refuse to keep my commandments and instructions? See! The LORD has given you the sabbath, therefore on the sixth day he gives you food for two days; each of you stay where you are; do not leave your place on the seventh day."
> So the people rested on the seventh day (vv. 25–30).

The conclusion affirmed by the narrative is that wherever YHWH governs as an alternative to Pharaoh, there the restfulness of YHWH effectively counters the restless anxiety of Pharaoh.

In our own contemporary context of the rat race of anxiety, the celebration of Sabbath is an act of both resistance and alternative. It is resistance because it is a visible insistence that our lives are not defined by the production and consumption of commodity goods. Such an act of resistance requires enormous intentionality and communal reinforcement amid the barrage of seductive pressures from the insatiable insistences of the market, with its intrusion into every part of our life from the family to the national budget. In our anxious society, to cite a case in point, one of the great "seductions of Pharaoh" is the fact that "soccer practice" invades the rest day. Families, largely contained in market ideology, think of themselves as helpless before the requirements of such commitment. In context it requires (or "would require," subjunctive, contrary to fact) enormous, communal resolve to resist the demand.

But Sabbath is not only resistance. It is alternative. It is an alternative to the demanding, chattering, pervasive presence of advertising and its great liturgical claim of professional sports that devour all our "rest time." The alternative on offer is the awareness and practice of the claim that we are situated on the receiving end of the gifts of God. To be so situated is a staggering option, because we are accustomed to being on the initiating end of all things. We neither expect nor even want a gift to be given, so inured are we to accomplishing and achieving and possessing. Thus I have come to think that the fourth commandment on sabbath is the most difficult and most urgent of the commandments in our society, because it summons us to intent and conduct that defies the most elemental requirements of a commodity-propelled society that specializes in control and entertainment, bread and circuses . . . along with anxiety and violence.

I have taken as a theme for this little book a familiar phrase from the teaching of Jesus in Mathew 11: There he contrasts the "heavy yoke" of his contemporary society with his "easy yoke" (vv. 29–30). That heavy yoke about which his listeners knew perhaps refers to the imposition of Rome and the demanding taxation of the empire, an endless tax to support military adventurism. It is equally possible that the yoke refers to the stringent requirements of establishment religion in which many could not qualify. Either way, empire or religion that colludes with empire, the requirements of acquiescent conduct were heavy. And Jesus, who resisted such a yoke, offered an alternative life of discipleship. Thus in our text, *discipleship* may concern the love of God and the love of neighbor, practices readily alternative to "making it" in the economic world of command performance.

And now, in the utterance of Jesus and in the practice of Jesus and his community, gifts are given! The gifts that are given lie outside the domain of empire and its colluding symbol systems. By appealing to Jesus, I do not suggest Christian preemption of this defining Jewish observance. Rather Jesus fully understood and commended the practice of his Jewish inheritance, which invites to restfulness.

This book is addressed exactly to those who are "weary and heavy laden," made so by the insatiable requirements of our society—in its taxation for the sake of imperialism, in its social conformity that urges doing more and having more (now perniciously embodied in "teaching to test"), in its frightened intent that there should be no "free lunch" for anyone, in its assumption that there is a technological resolution of every human problem, in its pathologies of greed and control.

I am glad to thank David Maxwell, who first invited me to write on Sabbath for his enterprise The Thoughtful Christian. I am equally grateful to Marianne Blickenstaff for her readiness to move from that initial publication with David to what is offered here. And I am pleased that the press has now added a study guide. I anticipate that such a study guide will give many readers better access to the issues to be faced concerning Sabbath. I am most grateful for the work of Martha Bettis Gee who has prepared the study guide. She has engaged the material in a most thoughtful way that will be of great benefit to readers of the study as they pursue these urgent issues.

I have found this study to be an important existential one for me. I know about the restless anxiety of not yet having done enough. I am glad to dedicate this book to the memory of my mother, Hilda, who knew more about work than about rest. Charles was her firstborn who died young, in his second year, before I was born. I learned more about a work ethic from my mother than I did about rest. But my growing up was plain and simple, close to the soil. There was in our home a natural restfulness imposed by the measures of rural life and my father's blessed garden. My mother would readily interrupt her Sabbath rest for the sake of any of her sons, most especially for Charles, whose precarious life required such attentiveness that she willingly gave.

I have come to think that the moment of giving the bread of Eucharist as gift is the quintessential center of the notion of Sabbath rest in Christian tradition. It is gift! We receive in gratitude. Imagine having a sacrament named "thanks"! We are on the receiving end, without accomplishment, achievement, or qualification. It is a gift, and we are grateful! That moment of gift is a peaceable alternative that many who are "weary and heavy-laden, cumbered with a load of care" receive gladly. The offer of free gift, faithful to Judaism, might let us learn enough to halt the dramatic anti-neighborliness to which our society is madly and uncritically committed. Fishbane concludes concerning the "Lord of Peace":

> This is dying within life for love of God. It is a divestment of will for God's sake—and the wonder of the world.[6]

Walter Brueggemann,
Columbia Theological Seminary

NOTES

1. There are, of course, many fine studies of the Sabbath by Christian interpreters. Among the best is Marva J. Dawn, *Keeping the Sabbath Wholly: Ceasing, Resting, Embracing, Fasting* (Grand Rapids: Eerdmans, 1989).
2. Abraham Heschel, *The Sabbath: Its Meaning for Modern Man* (New York: Farrar, Straus, Giroux, 1951).
3. Michael Fishbane, *Sacred Attunement: A Jewish Theology* (Chicago: University of Chicago Press, 2008).
4. Ibid., 124–25.
5. Ibid., 125–27.
6. Ibid., 128.

Chapter 1

SABBATH AND THE FIRST
COMMANDMENT

INTERPRETATION SERIES EDITOR PATRICK MILLER HAS
shrewdly observed that the fourth commandment on
Sabbath is the "crucial bridge" that connects the Ten
Commandments together.[1] The fourth commandment
looks back to the first three commandments and the
God who rests (Exod. 20:3–7). At the same time, the
Sabbath commandment looks forward to the last six
commandments that concern the neighbor (vv. 12–17);
they provide for rest alongside the neighbor. God, self,
and all members of the household share in common
rest on the seventh day; that social reality provides a
commonality and a coherence not only to the community of covenant but to the commandments of Sinai as
well. For that reason, it is appropriate in our study of
the Sabbath commandment to begin with a reflection

on the first commandment and, subsequently, to finish our work with a consideration of the tenth commandment that concludes the Decalogue.

The first commandments concern God, God's aniconic character, and God's name (Exod. 20:3–7). But when we consider the identity of this God, we are made immediately aware that the God who will brook no rival and who eventually will rest is a God who is embedded in a narrative; this God is not known or available apart from that narrative. The narrative matrix of YHWH, the God of Israel, is the exodus narrative. This is the God "who brought you out of the land of Egypt, out of the house of slavery" (v. 2). Thus the Sabbath commandment is drawn into the exodus narrative, for the God who rests is the God who emancipates *from slavery* and consequently *from the work system of Egypt* and *from the gods of Egypt* who require and legitimate that work system. It is, for that reason, fair to judge that the prohibition against "the other gods" in the first commandment pertains directly to the gods of Egypt (see Exod. 12:12) and other gods of the same ilk in Canaan, or subsequently the gods of the great empires of Assyria, Babylon, or Persia. In the narrative imagination of Israel, the gods of Egypt are stand-ins for all the gods of the several empires. What they all have in common is that they are confiscatory gods who demand endless produce and who authorize endless systems of production that are, in principle, insatiable. Thus, the mention of "Egypt" brings the God of Israel into the orbit of socioeconomic systems and practices, and inevitably sets this God on a collision course with the gods of insatiable productivity.

The reference to "Egypt" indicates that the God of Sinai who gives the Ten Commandments is never simply a "religious figure" but is always preoccupied with and attentive to socioeconomic practice and policy. If we want, then, to understand this God (or any god), we must look to the socioeconomic system that god legitimates and authorizes. In the case of the Egyptian gods (who are in contrast to and in competition with the God of the exodus), we look to Pharaoh's system of production that is legitimated by the gods worshiped by Pharaoh. In Exodus 5, we are given a passionate narrative account of that labor system in which Pharaoh endlessly demands more production. What the slaves are to produce is more bricks that are to be used for the building of more "supply cities" in which Pharaoh can store his endless supply of material wealth in the form of grain (see Exod. 1:11). Because the system was designed to produce more and more surplus (see Gen. 47:13–26), there is always more need for storage units that in turn generated more need for bricks with which to construct them. Thus, if we follow the required bricks from the slave camps, we end with surplus wealth, taken as a gift of the gods of Pharaoh.

In this narrative report, Pharaoh is a hard-nosed production manager for whom production schedules are inexhaustible:

- "[W]hy are you taking the people away from their work? Get to your labors!" (Exod. 5:4)
- ". . . yet you want them to stop working!" (v. 5)
- "You shall no longer give the people straw to

make bricks as before; let them go and gather straw for themselves. But you shall require of them the same quantity of bricks as they have made previously; do not diminish it, for they are lazy." (vv. 7–8)

– "Let heavier work be laid on them; then they will labor at it and pay no attention to deceptive words." (v. 9)

– "I will not give you straw. Go and get straw yourselves, wherever you can find it; but your work will not be lessened in the least." (vv. 10–11)

– "Complete your work the same daily assignment as when you were given straw." (v. 13)

– "Why did you not finish the required quantity of bricks yesterday and today, as you did before?" (v. 14)

– "No straw is given to your servants, yet they say to us, 'Make bricks.'" (v. 16)

– "You are lazy, lazy; that is why you say, 'Let us go and sacrifice to the Lord.' Go now, and work; for no straw will be given you but you shall still deliver the same number of bricks." (vv. 17–19)

– "You shall not lessen your daily number of bricks." (v. 19)

The rhetoric is relentless, all to the single point, as relentless as is the production schedule.

It is clear that in this system there can be no Sabbath rest. There is no rest for Pharaoh in his supervisory capacity, and he undoubtedly monitors daily production schedules. Consequently, there can be no rest for Pharaoh's supervisors or taskmasters; and of course there can be no rest for the slaves who must satisfy the taskmasters in order to meet Pharaoh's demanding quotas. We may imagine, moreover, that the "Egyptian gods" also never rested, because of their commitment to the aggrandizement of Pharaoh's system, for the glory of Pharaoh surely redounded to the glory of the Egyptian gods. The economy reflects the splendor of the gods who legitimate the entire system, for which cheap labor is an indispensable footnote!

It requires no imagination to see that the exodus memory and consequently the Sinai commandments are performed in a "no Sabbath" environment. In that context, all levels of social power—gods, Pharaoh, supervisors, taskmasters, slaves—are uniformly caught up in and committed to the grind of endless production.

Into this system of hopeless weariness erupts the God of the burning bush (Exod. 3:1–6). That God heard the despairing fatigue of the slaves (2:23–25), resolved to liberate the slave company of Israel from that exploitative system (3:7–9), and recruited Moses for the human task of emancipation (3:10). The reason Miriam and the other women can sing and dance at the end of the exodus narrative is the emergence of a new social reality in which the life of the Israelite economy is no longer determined and compelled by the insatiable production quotas of Egypt and its gods (15:20–21).

The first commandment is a declaration that the God of the exodus is *unlike* all the gods the slaves have known heretofore. This God is not to be confused with or thought parallel to the insatiable gods of imperial productivity. This God is subsequently revealed as a God of mercy, steadfast love, and faithfulness who is committed to covenantal relationships of fidelity (see Exod. 34:6–7). At the taproot of this divine commitment to *relationship (covenant)* rather than *commodity (bricks)* is the capacity and willingness of this God to rest. The Sabbath rest of God is the acknowledgment that God and God's people in the world are not commodities to be dispatched for endless production and so dispatched, as we used to say, as "hands" in the service of a command economy. Rather they are subjects situated in an economy of neighborliness. All of that is implicit in the reality and exhibit of divine rest.

Thus the Sabbath command of Exodus 20:11 recalls that God rested on the seventh day of creation, an allusion to Genesis 2:1–4. That divine rest on the seventh day of creation has made clear (a) that YHWH is not a workaholic, (b) that YHWH is not anxious about the full functioning of creation, and (c) that the well-being of creation does not depend on endless work. This performance and exhibit of divine rest thus characterize the God of creation, creation itself, and the creatures made in the image of the resting God. Creation is to be enacted and embraced without defining anxiety. Indeed, such divine rest serves to delegitimate and dismantle the endless restlessness sanctioned by the other gods and enacted by their adherents. That divine rest on the seventh day, moreover, is recalled in the commandment of Exodus 31:12–17, wherein God is "refreshed" on the seventh day. The God of Israel (and of creation) is no immovable, fixed object, but here is said to be depleted and by rest may recover a full sense of "self" (*nephesh*).

The second commandment is closely related to the first. The commandment against "graven images" (idols) is a prohibition against any artistic representation of YHWH, for such representation would serve to "locate" YHWH, to domesticate God and so to curb the freedom that belongs to this erupting God (Exod. 20:4–6; see 2 Sam. 7:6–7). Such images have the effect of drawing God, in imagination and in practice, away from covenantal, relational fidelity and back into a world of objects and commodities. The temptation to produce an "image" of God in artistic form is always, everywhere a chance to produce a commodity out of valuable material, at best gold if it is available, or lesser valuable material if there is no gold. When a god is fashioned into a golden commodity (or even lesser material), divine subject becomes divine object, and agent becomes commodity. We may cite two obvious examples of this temptation in the Old Testament. First, in the narrative of the "Golden Calf" in Exodus 32, it was gold that was fashioned into the image that readily became an alternative god who jeopardized the covenant. The ensuing narrative of Exodus 33–34 tells of the hard and tricky negotiations whereby covenantal possibility is restored to Israel after its foray into distorting images (Exod. 34:9–10). Less dramatically, it is evident that Solomon's temple, designed to "house" YHWH, became a commodity enterprise preoccupied with gold (emphasis added):

> The interior of the inner sanctuary was twenty cubits long, twenty cubits wide, and twenty cubits high; he overlaid it with pure *gold.* He also overlaid the altar

with cedar. Solomon overlaid the inside of the house with pure *gold,* then he drew chains of *gold* across in front of the inner sanctuary, and overlaid it with *gold.* Next he overlaid the whole house with *gold,* in order that the whole house might be perfect; even the whole altar that belonged to the inner sanctuary he overlaid with *gold.* (1 Kgs. 6:20–22)

So Solomon made all the vessels that were in the house of the LORD: the *golden* altar, the *golden* table for the bread of the Presence, the lampstands of pure *gold,* five on the south side and five on the north, in front of the inner sanctuary; the flowers, the lamps, and the tongs of *gold,* the cups, snuffers, basins, dishes for incense, and fire pans of pure *gold;* the sockets for the doors of the innermost part of the house, the most holy place, and for the doors of the nave of the temple of *gold.* (7:48–50)

Even as YHWH was honored by such extravagance, the temple was clearly intended to reflect honor on Solomon and on his regime. The attention to gold objects clearly skewed the simple and direct matter of covenantal possibility. Commodity desire has, for the most part, crowded out the covenantal tradition.

In the modern world, Karl Marx reflected most deeply on the compelling power of commodity. He took his famous phrase "commodity fetishism" from current study of the history of religions in which it was judged that "primitives" had such fetishes that occupied their desire and their devotion. Marx transferred that idea from "primitive" practice to modern market fascination and came to see that possessing commodities of social value generated a desire for more such value so that commodity took on a power of its own that consisted of desire for more and more. It is easy enough to see Pharaoh's compulsion for more grain (a measure of wealth) beyond anything he could have needed, simply so that he could exhibit his great wealth and power. His desire for more created a restlessness that could permit no Sabbath rest for himself or any in his domain. And clearly Solomon is sketched out as the one who would possess all of his available world in his insatiable need for more (see 1 Kgs. 10:14–25).

For good reason the book of Deuteronomy ponders the force and danger of "images of God." In what is likely a late exposition of the first two commandments, this sermonic chapter looks back to the danger done by "commodity religion":

> Since you saw no form when the LORD spoke to you at Horeb out of the fire, take care and watch yourselves closely, so that you do not act corruptly by making an idol for yourselves, in the form of any figure—the likeness of male or female, the likeness of any animal that is on the earth, the likeness of any winged bird that flies in the air, the likeness of anything that creeps on the ground, the likeness of any fish that is in the water under the earth. And when you look up to the heavens and see the sun, the moon, and the stars, all the host of heaven, do not be led astray and bow down to them and serve them, things that the LORD your God has allotted to all the peoples everywhere under heaven. (Deut. 4:15–19)

The danger is to compromise the peculiarity of YHWH and of Israel.

After this inventory of possible images, the rhetoric of verse 20 voices the alternative:

But the LORD has taken you and brought you out of
the iron-smelter, out of Egypt, to become a people of
his very own possession, as you are now.

The emancipatory gift of YHWH to Israel is
contrasted with all the seductions of images. The
memory of the exodus concerns the God of freedom
who frees. The clear implication is that fixed images
preclude freedom and become icons of stable equi-
librium. Such image-religion becomes a way of sustaining status quo socioeconomic power that negates
the emancipatory impulse of Israel's God and Israel's
defining narrative. Thus it is credible to see that the
culmination of *creation* in Sabbath and the culmination of *exodus* in Sabbath together refuse Pharaoh's
pursuit of commodity. This refusal is decisive for Israel's faith and Israel's management of the economy: Do
not worship such objects or make them your defining
desire! That radical either/or is precisely the issue of
the first commandment. It concerns the two tempta-
tions Israel faced, a temptation toward idols and an
economic temptation of Israel to commodity.

YHWH is a Sabbath-keeping God, which fact
ensures that restfulness and not restlessness is at the
center of life. YHWH is a Sabbath-giving God and a
Sabbath-commanding God. Israel, for that reason, is
always again to re-choose between "life and death"
(Deut. 30:15–20), between YHWH and "the gods of
your ancestors" (Josh. 24:14–15), between YHWH and
Baal (1 Kgs. 18:21), between the way of Torah and the
way of sinners (Ps. 1). Sabbath becomes a decisive, concrete, visible way of opting for and aligning with the
God of rest.

That same either/or is evident, of course, in the teaching of Jesus. In his Sermon on the Mount, he declares to his disciples:

> No one can serve two masters; for a slave will either hate the one and love the other, or be devoted to the one and despise the other. You cannot serve God and wealth. (Matt. 6:24)

The way of *mammon* (capital, wealth) is the way of commodity, which is the way of endless desire, endless productivity, and endless restlessness without any Sabbath. Jesus taught his disciples that they could not have it both ways.

In the tradition of Matthew, the next verses (vv. 25–33) exposit the power of anxiety as the alternative to trust. It is, of course, in the same gospel tradition that Jesus comes to these familiar words:

> Come to me, all you that are weary and are carrying heavy burdens, and I will give you rest. Take my yoke upon you, and learn from me; for I am gentle and humble in heart, and you will find rest for your souls. For my yoke is easy, and my burden is light. (11:28–30)

"Weariness, being heavy-laden, yoke" are all ways of speaking of the commodity society of endless productivity. In context, this might have referred to the strenuous taxation system of the Roman Empire, for "yoke" often refers to imperial imposition. Alternatively, this may have referred to the endless requirements of an over-coded religious system that required endless attentiveness. With reference to imperial imposition or over-coded religion, Jesus offers an alternative:

come to me and rest! He becomes the embodiment of Sabbath rest for those who are no longer defined by and committed to the system of productiveness. In this role he is, as he is characteristically, fully in sync with the tradition of Israel and with the Sabbath God who occupies that tradition.

Because Jews and Christians continue to attend to these commandments as contemporary mandates, we may consider the ways in which the first commandment (concerning the emancipatory God and no other) and the second commandment (concerning images as commodities) pertain to our common life. It is, of course, the case that the commandments always pertain to the constancy of the human condition and to gospel possibility. But we may more particularly consider the peculiar and immediate way in which the first two commandments pertain to our present circumstance. The "choice of gods" is, in context, a choice of restlessness or restfulness.

The reality of restlessness in our contemporary society is obvious and epidemic. The identification of that restlessness perhaps goes back to the categories of Martin Luther concerning "faith and works," with the accent on "works" indicating a need to produce, perform, and qualify for the goodness of God. It is an easy move to take that Reformation accent on "works" and see in our current social restlessness evidence of not yet being good enough or having done enough. Or perhaps such restlessness is rooted in the Enlightenment discovery of the individual and the emergent ideology of individualism that cuts us off from the buoyant sustenance of community and tradition. In that ideology, one is not only free to secure one's own future without answering to any other; one is also required to secure one's own future, because a laissez-faire economics mandates that one must sink or swim by one's own effort, and it is never enough simply to tread water.

These rootages in Reformation and Enlightenment categories have created a contemporary circumstance in our society that generates an endless pursuit of greater security and greater happiness, a pursuit that is always unsatisfied, because we have never gotten or done enough . . . yet. The gods ("other gods") of this system are the gods of market ideology that summon to endless desires and needs that are never met but that always require yet greater effort.

The various elements of that restlessness of "not enough yet" and "greater effort required" are evident everywhere. But they are grounded in a theological desire for an ultimate reality of total satiation that is no reality at all. That theological "mis-commitment" is apparent in economic performance that can never fully satisfy. Such an intrinsic and systemic inadequacy is a recognizable echo of the ancient Hebrew slaves, harassed by many supervisors and taskmasters who kept reminding them of the inadequacy of their production.

– *The advertising game*, the liturgy of consumerism in the service of market theology, always offers one more product for purchase, one more car, one more deodorant, one more prescription drug, one more cell phone, one more beer. The message is that the "product" will make one safe or simply acceptable. But the preliminary message is that one is not yet safe or not yet acceptable because one does not yet have the product. The production of "new and improved," the endless advance of style, and the always-new technology make old possessions inadequate and incomplete so that there is and must be an open-ended effort to satisfy the gods of commodity.

– In order to have economic leverage to pursue such commodity, *an educational advantage* is all but indispensable. As a result, there is a striving for improvement reflected in "teaching to the test" so that we may demonstrate not only competence but also superiority. Such a commoditization of education means that the study of tradition in artful, critical fashion is lost in the urge of test scores. In order that one may test well, moreover, there is an incessant pressure for admission to the right school and thus tutorial pressure to enhance performance.

– But because test scores are not sufficient for admission to the "best" educational programs, there must be *supplementary extracurricular activity.* This in turn requires constantly attentive parents who perform as chauffeurs to get to the next tennis or soccer or piano lesson so that a prospect for fun or nurture disappears into restlessness that becomes a process of accumulation of qualifying marks.

– And if young persons are cast as performers of social restlessness, the economy is a process of getting ahead or of staying even by the same route of accumulation. As a result, the restlessness becomes *a political effort* to own and control congress and court appointments in order that laws may be enacted concerning credit and tax arrangements and regulatory agencies to make way for predation by the strong and well-connected in their desire for more. That restlessness inevitably has resulted in many "left behind" who cannot compete due to poor circumstance or opportunity or a defeatism that properly assesses one's hopeless chances in a rapacious system. The outcome of such endless striving for more is a social arrangement of the safety and happiness of the few at the expense of the many, a replica of the "pyramid" of ancient Pharaoh.

– Such economic advantage and the unsustainable standard of living that it permits require *an expansive and aggressive military* in order to control resources and markets so that the world economy, reflected in the World Bank and the International Monetary Fund, is designed to keep the gains flowing to the top of the pyramid of power and success. It is not accidental that the best graphic portrayal of this arrangement is a pyramid, the supreme construction of Pharaoh's system. Those at the top of the pyramid require huge amounts of cheap labor at a parsimonious "minimum wage" to make such a life possible.

– This limitless pursuit of consumer goods (and the political, cultural, and military requirements that go with it) in the interest of satiation necessitates over-production and *abuse of the land,* and the squandering of limited supplies of oil and water. Thus, the environment is savaged by such restlessness; the ordering creation is skewed, perhaps beyond viability. It is long since forgotten that rest is the final marking of creator and creation.

– The totem for such restlessness is perhaps *professional sports* (with major college sports only a subset of professional sports). The endless carnival of those sports constitutes a dramatic affirmation of power, wealth,

and virility in which "victory" is accomplished by
many abusive exploitations, all in pursuit of winning
and being on top of the heap of the money game.
– And of course, every facet of this restlessness is
grounded in and produces anxiety that variously issues
in aggression and finally manifests in *violence*:

- violence expressed in military adventurism that
  enjoys huge "patriotic" support;
- violence against the earth that is signaled by overuse;
- violence in sports, now with evidence of "paid
  injuries";
- violence in the neighborhood, with guns now the
  icon of "violent security";
- violence against every vulnerable population,
  sexual aggression against the young and the "war
  on the poor," which is accomplished by law and
  by banking procedures.

It is impossible, is it not, to overestimate the level of
anxiety that now characterizes social relationships in
our society of acute restlessness? That violent restlessness makes neighborliness nearly impossible.

None of this is new; all of it is much chronicled
among us. All of it is as old as Pharaoh's Egypt. The
narrative of the exodus is not a "one off" miracle. The
portrayal of the slave camps of Egypt and the deliver-
ance of the exodus do not constitute an isolated miracle. The narrative is a rendering of recurring social
relationships legitimated by anti-neighborly gods who
give warrant, in the interest of commodity, to redefine
neighbors as slaves, threats, rivals, and competitors.

Only when we ponder the "other gods" and the systems they authorize can we appreciate the radical nature of these first two commandments. Into this arena of restlessness comes the God of rest who offers relief from that anxiety-producing system. This God has no hunger for commodities and does not legitimate commodity systems. This God is attentive rather to the cries of those "left behind" and comes to open futures by exit (exodus) from systems of restlessness into the restfulness of neighborliness.

The two commandments go beneath social performance and social appearance to the deep, elemental, defining issue of "God versus the gods." These gods of commoditization for the most part go unchallenged in our world. As a result, their exploitative systems go unchallenged and unnoticed. The abuse becomes normal. Restlessness is unexceptional. Anxiety is a given, and violence is unexamined as "the cost of doing business." It is all a virtual reality in which we become narcotized into a system that seems to be a given rather than a construction.

In that context, we have the exodus narrative that shows those gods of commodity to be powerless and without authority. They are phonies that we should neither fear nor serve nor trust:

> They have mouths, but do not speak;
>   eyes, but do not see.
> They have ears, but do not hear;
>   noses, but do not smell.
> They have hands, but do not feel;
>   feet, but do not walk;
> they make no sound in their throat. (Ps. 115:5–7)

More than that:

> Those who make them are like them;
> so are all who trust in them. (v. 8)

They are the ones who champion anxiety and affirm restlessness. The adherents to the gods of restlessness find such a predatory society normal.

And then into our midst comes this other unexpected voice from outside the Pharonic system: "Let my people go!" (Exod. 5:1). It is not surprising that Pharaoh does not recognize the commanding voice of YHWH. Pharaoh's system precludes and denies any such commanding voice that emancipates (v. 2). But YHWH persists: Let them go outside the system of restlessness that ends in violence. Let them depart the system of endless production, in order to enter a world of covenantal fidelity. In ancient context, they must depart from the Egyptian system in order to dance and sing freedom.

The departure from that same system in our time is not geographical. It is rather emotional, liturgical, and economic. It is not an idea but a practical act. Thus the Sabbath of the fourth commandment is an act of trust in the subversive, exodus-causing God of the first commandment, an act of submission to the restful God of commandments one, two, and three. Sabbath is a practical divestment so that neighborly engagement, rather than production and consumption, defines our lives. It is for good reason that Sabbath has long been, for theologically serious Jews, the defining discipline. It is also for good reason that Enlightenment-based autonomous Christians may find the Sabbath commandment the most urgent and the most difficult of all the commandments of Sinai. We are, liberals and conservatives, much inured to Pharaoh's system. For that reason, the departure into restfulness is both urgent and difficult, for our motors are set to run at brick-making speed. To cease, even for a time, the anxious striving for more bricks is to find ourselves with a "light burden" and an "easy yoke." It is now, as then, enough to permit dancing and singing into an alternative life.

NOTES

1. Patrick D. Miller, *The Ten Commandments*, Interpretation (Louisville, KY: Westminster John Knox Press, 2009), 117.

Chapter 2

RESISTANCE TO ANXIETY
Exodus 20:12–17

SABBATH-KEEPING IS A DISTINCTIVELY JEWISH ART FORM. It is, however, a practice and a discipline that has long preoccupied Christians who have responded to a core requirement of the God of covenant. It is unfortunate that in U.S. society, largely out of a misunderstood Puritan heritage, Sabbath has gotten enmeshed in legalism and moralism and blue laws and life-denying practices that contradict the freedom-bestowing intention of Sabbath. Such distortions, moreover, have led to endlessly wearying quarrels about "Sunday activities" such as movies and card playing and, currently in my state, purchasing liquor on Sunday.

All that common lore in U.S. society, of course, amounts to a pitiful misrepresentation of Sabbath-keeping as an art form. When taken seriously in faith by Jews—

and derivatively by Christians—Sabbath-keeping is a way
of making a statement of peculiar identity amid a larger
public identity, of maintaining and enacting a counter-
identity that refuses "mainstream" identity, which itself
entails anti-human practice and the worship of anti-
human gods. Understood in this way, Sabbath is a bodily
act of *testimony* to alternative and *resistance* to pervad-
ing values and the assumptions behind those values. In
these expositions, consideration will be given to Sabbath-
keeping as testimony and resistance, acts of faith com-
monly shared (in different forms) by Jews and Christians.

I

Our beginning point is the Sabbath command at Mount
Sinai in Exodus 20:8–11. Israel arrived at Mount Sinai
directly after it miraculously departed from the exploitative environment of Pharaoh's Egypt. Without knowing what would happen at the mountain with YHWH
or what it would be like to meet the emancipator God
of the exodus, Israel came to the mountain to enact
and acknowledge "regime change," an embrace of the
rule of the God of the covenant as an alternative to
the rule of Pharaoh, who was still so well remembered.
The regime change itself had been accomplished dramatically in the wonder of the exodus whereby YHWH
had acted in power and exposed Pharaoh as a weak
and failed governor. The departure from Egypt evoked
a great celebrative hymn from Israel that continues to
have echoes in Handel's M*essiah*:

The LORD will reign forever and ever. (Exod. 15:18)

Israel embraced the new governance, but then it had to receive and accept the new rules of governance that would enact the will and purpose of the new Governor in the world. That is what happened at Sinai. Israel received and swore allegiance to the new commands of YHWH that were in stark contrast to the commands of Pharaoh:

> Then he took the book of the covenant, and read it in the hearing of the people; and they said, "All that the LORD has spoken we will do, and we will be obedient." (24:7)

While there are other commands from YHWH at Sinai, the oath pertains centrally to the ten commandments (20:1–17). In that recital of new "policies," Israel is enjoined to "love God" in a singular way (20:3–7) and to "love neighbor" in respectful ways (20:12–17).

II

The utterance of the ten commandments by YHWH to Israel begins, amazingly enough, with reference to Pharaoh and to Egypt. The recent departure from Egypt, still vividly remembered, provides the context and urgency for the new rule of YHWH:

> I am the LORD your God, who brought you out of the land of Egypt, out of the house of slavery. (20:2)

All parties at Sinai—YHWH, Moses, Israel—could well remember what it had been like in the world of Pharaoh:

- They could remember that Pharaoh was regarded, and regarded himself, as a god, an absolute authority who was thought to be immune to the vagaries of history, a force with insatiable demands.
- They could remember that Egypt's socioeconomic power was organized like a pyramid, with a workforce producing wealth, all of which flowed upward to the power elite and eventually to Pharaoh who sat atop that pyramid.
- They could remember that Pharaoh, even though he was absolute in authority and he occupied the pinnacle of power, was an endlessly anxious presence who caused the entire social environment to be permeated with a restless anxiety that had no limit or termination.
- They could remember that Pharaoh, who controlled the Nile, nevertheless had nightmares of anxiety, as he dreamed of famine and as he imagined that the creation would not produce sufficient food (Gen. 41:15–32).
- They could remember how that nightmare of scarcity, which contradicted the wealth and power of Pharaoh, led to rapacious state policies of monopoly that caused the crown to usurp the money, the cattle, the land, and, finally, the bodies of vulnerable peasants (47:13–26).
- They could remember that such exploitative policies eventually reduced the peasants to state slaves, who were kept busy building granaries to store the vast food supplies of the state monopoly (Exod. 1–11).
- They could remember that the frantic policies of

Pharaoh, based on anxiety about food production, would lead to heavy-handed misery and the need to keep working and keep producing in order to meet insatiable imperial quotas that were without end.

- They could remember all of that when the God of Sinai announced God's self as the one "who brought you out of the land of Egypt, out of the house of slavery."

<h1 style="text-align:center">III</h1>

Pharaoh was remembered at Sinai. But Pharaoh was not at Sinai. He was left helpless and disabled at the bottom of the waters (15:4–10). At Sinai, while Pharaoh was remembered, YHWH was front and center as the decisive force who enwrapped Israel in new promises and new social possibilities. Israel was so eager to trade off Pharaoh's hopeless commands and requirements for those of YHWH that, even before they heard the new commands, they gladly swore their readiness to sign on for the new regime:

> The people all answered as one: "Everything that the LORD has spoken we will do." Moses reported the words of the people to the LORD. (19:8)

Without knowing what would be required they had no doubt it would be better than the demands of Pharaoh.

And then God spoke ten times in the midst of fire and smoke.

God spoke three times in self-regard with a claim of exclusiveness:

I am the Lord your God, who brought you out of the land of Egypt, out of the house of slavery; you shall have no other gods before me.

You shall not make for yourself an idol, whether in the form of anything that is in heaven above, or that is on the earth beneath, or that is in the water under the earth. You shall not bow down to them or worship them; for I the Lord your God am a jealous God, punishing children for the iniquity of parents, to the third and the fourth generation of those who reject me, but showing steadfast love to the thousandth generation of those who love me and keep my commandments.

You shall not make wrongful use of the name of the Lord your God, for the Lord will not acquit anyone who misuses his name. (20:2–7)

This claim of exclusiveness sounded at first like the exclusive claim of Pharaoh, for Pharaoh also required absolute authority without any rival. But the exclusivity of YHWH was different because of what followed.

God spoke six times about the neighbor:

Honor your father and your mother, so that your days may be long in the land that the Lord your God is giving you.

You shall not murder.

You shall not commit adultery.

You shall not steal.

You shall not bear false witness against your neighbor.

You shall not covet your neighbor's house; you shall not covet your neighbor's wife, or male or female slave, or ox, or donkey, or anything that belongs to your neighbor. (vv. 12–17)

This terse summary was quite unlike any decree of Pharaoh, because it includes the neighbor in the social calculus and dares to imagine the maintenance of a neighborly community. It was not so in Egypt. There were no neighbors in that system, only threats and competitors. In his continued interpretation of the commands, Moses spoke more about the most vulnerable of the neighbors who receive attentive consideration and protection by the Lord of the covenant:

> You shall not wrong or oppress a resident alien, for you were aliens in the land of Egypt. You shall not abuse any widow or orphan. If you do abuse them, when they cry out to me, I will surely heed their cry; my wrath will burn, and I will kill you with the sword, and your wives shall become widows and your children orphans. (22:21–24)

> If you lend money to my people, to the poor among you, you shall not deal with them as a creditor; you shall not exact interest from them. If you take your neighbor's cloak in pawn, you shall restore it before the sun goes down; for it may be your neighbor's only clothing to use as cover; in what else shall that person sleep? And if your neighbor cries out to me, I will listen, for I am compassionate. (vv. 25–27)

> You shall not oppress a resident alien; you know the heart of an alien, for you were aliens in the land of Egypt. (23:9)

These folk are put at the center of Sinai imagination, even though they are nowhere in the horizon of the Egyptian system.

But that posed a deep question for those fresh from Egypt. How does one regard the neighbor seriously when one has imbibed the profound anxiety of the Egyptian system? If one is a slave, one has anxiety about the brick quotas. If one is a Pharaoh, one is anxious about the food monopoly. In fact, Pharaoh and slave colluded in a common enterprise that made neighborliness impossible. To that issue, YHWH spoke one more time from the fiery mountain and placed this utterance exactly between the exclusivity of YHWH and the production of the neighbor:

> Remember the Sabbath day, and keep it holy. Six days you shall labor and do all your work. But the seventh day is a Sabbath to the LORD your God; you shall not do any work—you, your son or your daughter, your male or female slave, your livestock, or the alien resident in your towns. For in six days the LORD made heaven and earth, the sea, and all that is in them, but rested the seventh day and consecrated it. (20:8–11)

How strange to use the most airtime at the mountain on the Sabbath command. The divine utterance must have come as a shock to the listening Israelites. There had been no Sabbath in Egypt, no work stoppage; no work stoppage for Pharaoh who worked day and night to stay atop the pyramid. There had been no work stoppage for the slaves, because they had to gather straw during their time off; no work stoppage of anybody in the Egyptian system, because frantic productivity drove the entire system. And now YHWH nullifies that entire system of anxious production. There are limits to how much and how long slaves must produce bricks! There are limits to how much food Pharaoh can store and consume and administer. The limit is set by the weekly work pause that breaks the production cycle. And those who participate in it break the anxiety cycle. They are invited to awareness that life does not consist in frantic production and consumption that reduces everyone else to threat and competitor. And as the work stoppage permits a waning of anxiety, so energy is redeployed to the neighborhood. The odd insistence of the God of Sinai is to counter *anxious productivity* with *committed neighborliness*. The latter practice does not produce so much; but it creates an environment of security and respect and dignity that redefines the human project.

IV

Perhaps someone would ask for a basis for work stoppage that contradicts the core enterprise of the economic rat race. YHWH, at the mountain, anticipates such a question and answers:

> For in six days the LORD made heaven and earth, the sea, and all that is in them, but rested the seventh day and consecrated it. (20:11)

God rested! God enjoyed a work stoppage! The verse is a direct reference to the creation liturgy of Genesis 1:1–2:4a. In that well-known liturgical recital, the world begins in chaos, "formless and void." The narrative account reviews the steady pace of God's creative activity in taming and ordering chaos and making viable life in the world possible. The verses articulate the way in which God ordered the world to be fruitful and generative and the way in which God substantiated the power of blessing in the intrinsic ordering of creation. And the congregation responds in the recital with the repeated formula, "It is good." It is good that order defeats chaos. It is good that the world is ordered for fruitfulness. It is "very good" that creation bears the life-giving power of the creator. It is very good indeed!

And then, reported as the culmination of the liturgical recital, God rested. God rested on the seventh day. God did not show up to do more. God absented God's self from the office. God did not come and check on creation in anxiety to be sure it was all working. God has complete confidence in the fruit-bearing, blessing-generating processes of creation that have been instituted. God exhibits no anxiety about the life-giving capacity of creation. God knows the world will hold, the plants will perform, and the birds and the fish and the beasts of the field will prosper. Humankind will govern the earth in a generative way. All will be well, and all manner of thing will be well!

Israel, in its many songs, voices complete confidence in the food-producing, life-assuring potential of the earth:

> These all look to you
>   to give them their food in due season;
> when you give to them, they gather it up;
>   when you open your hand,
> they are filled with good things. (Ps. 104:27–28)

> The eyes of all look to you,
>   and you give them their food in due season.
> You open your hand,
>   satisfying the desire of every living thing.
>   (145:15–16)

The world is an anxiety-free one of well-being because the creator is anxiety-free and publicly exhibits that freedom from anxiety by not checking things out. God is not a workaholic. God is not a Pharaoh. God does not keep jacking up production schedules. To the contrary, God rests, confident, serene, at peace. God's rest, moreover, bestows on creatureliness a restfulness that contradicts the "drivenness" of the system of Pharaoh.

V

Moses at Sinai says to the new post–Pharaoh community of covenant:

> Remember the Sabbath day, and keep it holy. Six days you shall labor and do all your work. But the seventh day is a Sabbath to the LORD your God; you shall not do any work—you, your son or your daughter, your male or female slave, your livestock, or the alien resident in your towns. For in six days the LORD made heaven and earth, the sea, and all that is in them, but rested the seventh day and consecrated it. (Exod. 20:8–11)

Rest as did the creator God! And while you rest, be sure that your neighbors rest alongside you. Indeed, sponsor a *system of rest* that contradicts the *system of anxiety* of Pharaoh, because you are no longer subject to Pharaoh's anxiety system. Create restfulness with theological rootage, political viability, and economic significance for all in the domain of covenant—all sons and daughters, all slaves, all cattle, all immigrants, all who depart the death system of Pharaoh—who engage the offer of life given in covenant. Those who live by the death system:

- are bound to dishonor parents and all non-productive kin;

- are bound to engage in killing violence, because the others are a threat;
- are bound to reduce sexual interaction to exploitative commodity;
- are bound to usurp from others if it is something they want;
- are bound to engage in distortion and euphemism to gain advantage;
- are bound to be committed to acquisitiveness.

Moses recited all the commandments. You who keep Sabbath do not need

- to dishonor mother and father,
- to kill,
- to commit adultery,
- to steal,
- to bear false witness,
- to covet.

You do not need to because you are able to depart the exploitative system.

So imagine, says Moses at Sinai, you who engage in production and consumption are not little replicas of anxiety-driven Pharaoh. You are in the image of the creator God who did not need to work to get ahead. Nor do you! God invites the ones at Sinai to a new life of neighborly freedom in which Sabbath is the cornerstone of faithful freedom. Such faithful practice of work stoppage is an act of resistance. It declares in bodily ways that we will not participate in the anxiety system that pervades our social environment. We will not be defined

by busyness and by acquisitiveness and by pursuit of
more, in either our economics or our personal relations
or anywhere in our lives. Because our life does not consist in commodity.

It is no wonder that Jesus invited his disciples out
of the anxiety system:

> Therefore I tell you, do not worry about your life,
> what you will eat or what you will drink, or about
> your body, what you will wear. Is not life more than
> food, and the body more than clothing? Look at the
> birds of the air; they neither sow nor reap nor gather
> into barns, and yet your heavenly Father feeds them.
> Are you not of more value than they? And can any
> of you by worrying add a single hour to your span
> of life? And why do you worry about clothing? Con-
> sider the lilies of the field, how they grow; they nei-
> ther toil nor spin, yet I tell you, even Solomon in all
> his glory was not clothed like one of these. But if
> God so clothes the grass of the field, which is alive
> today and tomorrow is thrown into the oven, will
> he not much more clothe you—you of little faith?
> Therefore do not worry, saying, "What will we eat?"
> or "What will be drink?" or "What will we wear?"
> (Matt. 6:25–31)

The birds and the lilies are attestation that creation
works! Trust it and live out righteousness, and your
"heavenly Father"—the creator—will see to your well-
being. Behind the sermon away from anxiety by Jesus
is the good word of Moses:

> Six days you shall do your work, but on the seventh
> day you shall rest, so that your ox and your donkey
> may have relief, and your homeborn slave and the res-
> ident alien may be refreshed. Be attentive to all that
> I have said to you. Do not invoke the names of other

gods; do not let them be heard on your lips. (Exod. 23:12–13)

The "other gods" are agents and occasions of anxiety. But we, by discipline, by resolve, by baptism, by Eucharist, and by passion, resist such seductions. In so doing we stand alongside the creator in whose image we are made. By the end of six days God had done all that was necessary for creation . . . so have we!

Chapter 3

RESISTANCE TO COERCION

Deuteronomy 5:12–14

AT SINAI, ISRAEL MADE A DEFINING CHOICE. IT DECIDED TO
trust the God who made heaven and earth (Exod.
20:11), to rely on the guaranteed reliabilities of the creation, and to eschew the anxiety that comes from loss
of confidence in the sureness of the creator and the
goodness of creation.

I

That defining choice, however, was not easy to sustain. The oath of allegiance to YHWH is sworn in
Exodus 24. But by Exodus 32, when Moses had been
gone from them for forty days and nights (see 24:18),
the God of the covenant seemed remote, and they fell

back to anxiety. The God who was their guarantor against anxiety seemed absent.

And so they acted in their acute anxiety. They gathered their gold (what else?), their precious earrings, their most treasured, coveted commodity, and they made their own god. They imagined that with a rightly honored commodity they could "purchase" security in a world that seemed devoid of the creator. "God-making" amid anxiety is a standard human procedure!

But of course, such god-making of *ersatz* gods evoked great anger on the part of the creator of heaven and earth. As a consequence of such anxious behavior, Moses broke the tablets of Sinai and the covenant was dissolved. Israel was for an instant hopeless, and Moses was bereft. In Exodus 32–34, Moses bargained with YHWH, prayed, and postured. In response to Moses' insistence, the God who nullified the covenant committed an enormous act of forgiveness. Even beyond Israel's disobedient anxiety, YHWH was prepared to begin again:

> He said: I hereby make a covenant. Before all your people I will perform marvels, such as have not been performed in all the earth or in any nation; and all the people among whom you live shall see the work of the LORD; for it is an awesome thing that I will do with you. (34:10)

Pursuant to a new covenant with this anxious people, YHWH does not here reiterate the ten commandments of Exodus 20 but instead offers a new regimen of commands (34:11–26). Of the new commands, there is only slight overlap with "The Big Ten." But among those that overlap, notice this reiteration:

> Six days you shall work, but on the seventh day you shall rest; even in plowing time and in harvest time you shall rest. (34:21)

Here there is no mention of the creator God. It is a command given without encouragement or motivation. But notice as well, the Sabbath here commanded pertains especially to "plowing time" and to "harvest time." That is, it concerns the human work of exercising "dominion" over the earth to cause it to produce (see Gen. 1:28). Sabbath is in the context of the productive, food-producing creation system in which human beings must participate. They must participate, but they are to trust the land—creation—enough to rest, even in the busy agricultural seasons of sowing and reaping; human life is to conform to the rhythms of creation. And when human persons are in sync with that, they can rest and be free from anxiety.

II

Then, with the broken covenant restored and Sabbath continuing to be a core commandment, Israel left Sinai. Eventually they came to the Jordan River, ready to enter—at long last—the promised land. But it was a long time since Sinai. And so, Moses stops at the Jordan—in the book of Deuteronomy—and gives Israel instruction for the new land, instruction that lasts for thirty chapters. Moses speaks so long because he regards the move into the new land as a high-risk venture. He wants to be sure that Israel understands that the old, desert covenant still pertains to the agricultural territory they are about to enter, a land that is claimed as well by other gods who are inimical to YHWH. Moses regards the land of Canaan, it being so fertile, as an enormous temptation and a huge seduction to Israel. Moses knows that the affluence of the land is sure to create a crisis in covenant faith.

–The new land will work so well that Israel will think they can manage on their own. They will be tempted to autonomy, without due reference to YHWH. And the reason they will be tempted by autonomy is that the new land will make them inordinately prosperous. Moses knows that *prosperity breeds amnesia.* He warns Israel about amnesia:

> [T]ake care that you do not forget the LORD, who brought you out of the land of Egypt, out of the house of slavery. (6:12)

> [T]hen do not exalt yourself, forgetting the LORD your God, who brought you out of the land of Egypt, out of the house of slavery. (8:14)

The Israelites might forget where they came from, the circumstance they had departed, and how they had gotten away. They might forget that they had lived in a system of unbearable coercion wherein they had to meet impossible production schedules of more bricks. Moses anticipates that if they are not alert to the God of emancipation, they will end up right back in another system of coercion. Because the land is fertile, its produce will make Israel safe and happy. And if Israel can increase its produce, it will be safer and happier. And Israel will discover that the sky is the limit! The fertility of the land and the productivity of the system will make Israel acquisitive; Israel will come to think that the goal of its life is to acquire and acquire and acquire. And in order to acquire, Israelites must compete with the neighbor. The system will turn one's neighbor into a competitor and a threat and a challenge. Moses warns Israel to "Watch out!" or the land in its productivity will transform Israelites into producers and consumers and will destroy the fabric of the covenantal neighborhood.

– Moses understands, as do the prophets after him, that being in the land poses for Israel a conflict between two economic systems, each of which views the land differently. On the one hand, the land is regarded as property and possession to be bought and sold and traded and used. On the other hand, in a context of covenant, the land is a birthright and an inheritance, one's own land as a subset of the larger inheritance of the whole people of God. If the land is possession, then the proper way of life is to acquire more. If the land is inheritance, then the proper way of life is to enhance the neighborhood and the extended family so that all members may enjoy the good produce of the land. It is clear which of these perspectives was appropriate to Sinai. But in its amnesia, Israel may forget its covenantal frame of reference and generate an economy that is anti-neighborly in order to have more and more.

– And so, in his great interpretive maneuver, Moses asserts:

The LORD our God made a covenant with us at Horeb.
Not with our ancestors did the LORD make this covenant, but with us, who are all of us here alive today.
(5:2–3)

Moses remembers the ancient covenant of Sinai
(Horeb) made to a previous generation in Israel. But
then, in a series of words that Moses piles up—"all
of us, here, alive, this day"—the covenant is said to
be immediately contemporary for the new generation.
This is the core argument of the book of Deuteronomy, the center of covenantal teaching in the Bible.
The economy is not a rat race in which people remain
exhausted from coercive goals; it is, rather, a covenantal
enterprise for the sake of the whole community. Even
in a new circumstance of agricultural possibility, the
old desert covenant is defining. Moses expects Israel
to reject the acquisitive culture of its neighbors for the
sake of a covenantal alternative.

III

To this end, Moses articulates the commandments,
moving from "no other gods" to "do not covet" (5:6–
21). The commandments are the same as the Sinai
recital in Exodus 20, with only slight variation. The
actual commandment is the same as that voiced at
Sinai:

Observe the Sabbath day and keep it holy, as the LORD
your God commanded you. Six days you shall labor
and do all your work. But the seventh day is a Sabbath
to the LORD your God; you shall not do any work—
you, or your son or your daughter, or your male or

female slave, or your ox or your donkey, or any of
your livestock, or the resident alien in your towns, so
that your male and female slave may rest as well as
you. (5:12–14)

Even in this part of the command, however, there
is one noteworthy change. As in Exodus 20, all are to
rest: "sons and daughters, slaves, oxen, donkeys, livestock, immigrants." But a phrase is added, "that they
may rest *like you*." Sabbath is the great day of equal-
ity when all are equally at rest. Not all are equal in
production. Some perform much more effectively than
others. Not all are equal in consumption. Some have
greater access to consumer goods. In a society defined
by production and consumption, there are huge gradations of performance and, therefore, of worth and significance. In such a social system, everyone is coerced
to perform better—produce more, consume more—
be a good shopper! Such valuing, of course, creates
"haves" and "have-nots," significant and insignificant,
rich and poor, people with access and people denied
access.

But Sabbath breaks that gradation caused by coercion. On the Sabbath:

- You do not have to do more.
- You do not have to sell more.
- You do not have to control more.
- You do not have to know more.
- You do not have to have your kids in ballet or
  soccer.
- You do not have to be younger or more beautiful.
- You do not have to score more.

Because this one day breaks the pattern of coercion, all are *like you*, equal—equal worth, equal value, equal access, equal rest. The motivational clause for the Sabbath command includes a momentous variation from the Sinai version of the command. We recall that at Sinai it was a command to rest, for the creator rested on the seventh day. But not here. Here the motivation for Sabbath is not creation. Moses in Deuteronomy says to rest:

> Remember that you were a slave in the land of Egypt, and the LORD your God brought you out from there with a mighty hand and an outstretched arm; therefore the LORD your God commanded you to keep the Sabbath day. (5:15)

Remember the exodus! Remember that the coercive system of Pharaoh was disrupted. Remember that the brick quota was declared null and void. Moses warned the Israelites: if you forget this, you will give your life over to coercive competition. But if you remember, you will know that Pharaoh and all like agents of coercion have been defeated. You do not need to meet expectations of your mother or your work or your boss or your broker or anybody else. You are free from the quota . . . if you remember, if you situate yourself in the covenant memory.

In Deuteronomy, Moses is very big on remembering, because he knows that forgetting is a huge temptation in an affluent environment. He knows that the aim of the market ideology (as of the casino) is to have us forget our rootage and our identity and to let ourselves be defined by alien expectations. So says Moses:

- "Just remember what the LORD your God did to Pharaoh and all Egypt." (7:18)
- "Remember the LORD your God, for it is he who gives you power to get wealth." (8:18)
- "Eat unleavened bread . . . because you came out of the land of Egypt in great haste, so that all the days of your life you may remember the day of your departure from the land of Egypt." (16:3)
- "Remember that you were a slave in Egypt, and diligently observe these statutes." (16:12)
- "Remember that you were slaves in Egypt, and the LORD your God rescued you from there; therefore I command you to do this." (24:18)
- "Remember that you were a slave in the land of Egypt; therefore I am commanding you to do this." (24:22)

Remember that the pattern of coercion has been broken. Do you, when you wake up in the night, remember what you were supposed to have done, vexed that you did not meet expectations? Do you fall asleep counting bricks? Do you dream of more bricks you have to make yet or of bricks you have made that were flawed? We dream so because we have forgotten the exodus!

Well . . . Sabbath is the break, regular and public, that permits us to remember. Sabbath is the opportunity to recall Egypt and Pharaoh and then to remember YHWH and exodus. Sabbath is the day to dance and sing, "Free at last, free at last," "Nobody gonna turn me around!" Those who remember and keep Sabbath find they are less driven, less coerced, less frantic to meet deadlines, free to be, rather than to do. Because Sabbath is the great festival of freedom, when Pharaoh and all coercive expectations are dismissed and there is free bread and free water and free milk and free wine:

> Ho, everyone who thirsts,
>   come to the waters;
> and you that have no money,
>   come, buy and eat!
> Come, buy wine and milk
>   without money and without price. (Isa. 55:1)

And then, in light of such free gifts, the poet asks the dreaded question:

> Why do you spend your money for that which is not
>   bread,
>   and your labor for that which does not satisfy?
> Listen carefully to me, and eat what is good,
>   and delight yourselves in rich food. (v. 2)

Why indeed? Because Pharaoh looms large in our imagination. But he need not! The free time lets us re-decide about coercion.

IV

Moses, in Deuteronomy, imagines that Sabbath is not only a festival day but also a new social reality that is carried back into days one through six. People who keep Sabbath live all seven days differently. So the task, according to Moses, is to "seven" our lives. We may identify two aspects of the new life made possible when patterns of coercion are broken by the faithful observance of Sabbath as a day of deep freedom.

First, in Deuteronomy 15:1–18, Moses enunci-
ates the most radical extrapolation of Sabbath in the
entire Bible. Every seven years, in an enactment of "the
sabbatic principle," Israel is enjoined to cancel debts
on poor people. The intention in this radical act of
"seven" is that there should be no permanent underclass in Israel (v. 4). Moses, in this instruction, anticipates resistance to the radical extrapolation of Sabbath,
that Israelites may be "hard hearted" and "tight fisted"
(v. 7). But that is because they have fallen into coercive
patterns whereby the poor are targeted as objects of
economic abuse rather than seen as Sabbath neighbors.
Moses counters such resistance, however, by appeal to
the exodus memory (v. 15). On the basis of that Sabbath memory, Israel is invited to "give liberally" (v. 10)
and "provide liberally" (v. 14).

Second, the great "triad of vulnerability" in the
book of Deuteronomy identifies widows, orphans, and
immigrants as needy members of society who are without protected rights. The tradition of Deuteronomy is
particularly attentive to their needs:

> You shall not deprive a resident alien or an orphan
> of justice; you shall not take a widow's garment in
> pledge. Remember that you were a slave in Egypt and
> the LORD your God redeemed you from there; there-
> fore I command you to do this.
>
> When you reap your harvest in your field and
> forget a sheaf in the field, you shall not go back to
> get it; it shall be left for the alien, the orphan, and
> the widow, so that the LORD your God may bless you
> in all your undertakings. When you beat your olive
> trees, do not strip what is left; it shall be for the alien,
> the orphan, and the widow.

When you gather the grapes of your vineyard,
do not glean what is left; it shall be for the alien, the
orphan, and the widow. Remember that you were a
slave in the land of Egypt; therefore I am commanding you to do this. (24:17–22)

It is no stretch at all to see that on Sabbath day these
vulnerable, exposed neighbors shall be "like you,"
peaceably at rest.

In this interpretive tradition, Sabbath is not simply
a pause. It is an occasion for reimagining all social life
away from coercion and competition to compassionate
solidarity. Such solidarity is imaginable and capable of
performance only when the drivenness of acquisitiveness is broken. Sabbath is not simply the pause that
refreshes. It is the pause that transforms. Whereas Israelites are always tempted to acquisitiveness, Sabbath is
an invitation to receptivity, an acknowledgment that
what is needed is given and need not be seized.

Chapter 4

RESISTANCE TO EXCLUSIVISM

Isaiah 56:3–8

ISRAEL IN THE OLD TESTAMENT IS ENDLESSLY SELF-conscious about its own identity and continually reflects on its distinctive role as a historical people. Israel is characteristically aware, at the same time, of its theological rootage according to the faithfulness of YHWH and its historical concreteness that relates to socioeconomic, territorial, and political realities. Its text traditions attest to the ways in which Israel continually negotiates its theological and historical destiny.

I

The formation of Israel is narrated as a process whereby YHWH's power transformed "no people" into "this people":

– The Hebrews, as forerunners of Israel, were treated, according to the tradition, as marginal, objectionable people. Indeed, in the Joseph narrative they were regarded as a threat to social propriety and kept separated from those who managed social power:

> They served him by himself, and them by themselves, and the Egyptians who ate with him by themselves, because the Egyptians could not eat with the Hebrews, for that is an abomination to the Egyptians. (Gen. 43:32)

That treatment is not unlike the way in which Whites have characteristically treated Blacks in U.S. society.

– In the exodus narrative it is remembered that Israel, in its departure from Egypt, was a "mixed multitude," not a readily identified population (Exod. 12:38).

– At Sinai, however, this gathering of disparate populations was formed and transformed by the will of YHWH into an identifiable, intentional community, called to a historical destiny:

> Now therefore, if you obey my voice and keep my covenant, you shall be my treasured possession out of all the peoples. Indeed, the whole earth is mine, but you shall be for me a priestly kingdom and a holy nation. These are the words that you shall speak to the Israelites. (19:5–6)

The wonder of the people of God in the Old Testament is the marvel of transformation whereby "not a people" became "God's people" (see 1 Pet. 2:10).

– Prophetic tradition remembered that transformative miracle of identity. On the one hand, Israel could imagine its becoming, yet again, "not my people" (Hos. 1:9).

But, on the other hand, it also trusted divine fidelity to cause them to become always anew, "my people" (Hos. 2:23). The identity of Israel as YHWH's people is a treasured claim, but one permeated with risk. For that reason, Israel always contested its identity, its destiny, and, consequently, its membership.

II

After the wonder of Exodus-Sinai and the doxological expression of that wonder, it did not take very long for Israel, in its traditioning process, to try to give order to its life and to establish boundaries of membership, to determine who was in and who was not. In general it is right to say that the "insiders," the legitimate members of this community of YHWH, are those who keep Torah, who obey the commandments of Sinai, and who swear allegiance to these commandments. Joshua 24 presents a liturgical occasion whereby a subsequent generation that was never at Sinai replicated Sinai, reiterated the oath of allegiance, and signed on as Israel:

> He said, "Then put away the foreign gods that are among you, and incline your hearts to the LORD, the God of Israel." The people said to Joshua, "The LORD our God we will serve, and him we will obey." So Joshua made a covenant with the people that day, and made statutes and ordinances for them at Shechem. (Josh. 24:23–25)

It is plausible to imagine that over time Israel reenacted this drama many times, always again incorporating new members into the community of Torah.

That practice of Torah whereby Israel received

and sustained its identity as the people of YHWH is expressed in the two great interpretive traditions of Torah. First, there is the great Priestly tradition of holiness voiced in the book of Leviticus that summoned Israel to be a holy people:

> Speak to all the congregation of the people of Israel and say to them: You shall be holy, for I the LORD your God am holy. (Lev. 19:2)

That tradition calls Israel to cultic purity, to stay clear of all that is profane and worldly, and common, because such exposures would contaminate Israel and drive YHWH out of Israel's presence. The book of Leviticus, in careful detail, provides guidelines for every phase of life to be sure that membership in Israel consists only in those who sustain intentional purity. Others are excluded because they jeopardize the entire community.

The second great interpretive tradition, Deuteronomy, takes the Sinai commandments in a somewhat different direction. It places accent on justice questions and is preoccupied with the vulnerable who need protection by the community: the poor, alongside widows, orphans, and immigrants. Israel consists in those who practice such protective justice:

> You must not distort justice; you must not show partiality; and you must not accept bribes, for a bribe blinds the eyes of the wise and subverts the cause of those who are in the right. Justice, and only justice, you shall pursue, so that you may live and occupy the land that the LORD your God is giving you. (Deut. 16:19–20)

In Deuteronomy, as in the Priestly tradition, purity is a continuing concern alongside justice:

You are the children of the LORD your God. You must not lacerate yourselves or shave your forelocks for the dead. For you are a people holy to the LORD your God; it is you the LORD has chosen out of all the peoples on earth to be his people, his treasured possession. (14:1–2)

Verses 3–21 follow this statement, moreover, with a long inventory of "clean and unclean" foods. All this data pertains to membership in the community.

In the tradition of Deuteronomy, the most interesting text on "membership" is the list of exclusions that Moses declares in Deuteronomy 23:1–8. The text is divided into two parts. First, in verses 1–2, Moses excludes from membership those with distorted genitalia, as though proper functioning of genitalia had become a condition of joining the community. It is likely that the accent on testicles and penises relates to the fruitful transmission of sperm in the maintenance of "the holy seed" (see Ezra 9:2; Neh. 9:2). Alongside that, in verse 2, bastards who are not "properly born" are excluded. The two verses enunciate criteria of right sexual relations as precondition of membership.

In the second part of the text, verses 3–8, Moses presents a checklist of non-Israelites. On the one hand, Ammonites and Moabites are unwelcome, with reference to ancient memories in the book of Numbers. Remarkably their "peace and prosperity" are never to be a concern for Israel. Since "peace and prosperity" are a cultic gift in that ancient community, they are excluded from Israel's worship and so cannot receive covenant blessing from either God or neighbor. By contrast, Edomites and Egyptians are to be

included in the community, a quite astonishing allow-
ance. Edomites are "kin" ("brothers"), remembered
according to the ancient connection to Esau. (Interest-
ingly, in Gen. 19:30–38, Ammon and Moab are also
"kin," but that point is not observed here.) Egyptians
are welcome on very different grounds, by appeal to
Israel's own memory of being outsiders in Egypt. One
might conclude that this distinction of those "in" and
those "out" is arbitrary, but so Moses declares. (This
is not the last time such distinctions would be arbitrary!) It is evident in this passage that "membership"
is a most serious matter, freighted with good and bad
memories; rigorous conditions must be met in order to
gain admission to the community.

In addition to this text on exclusive membership,
we may also notice the "formula of excommunication"
frequently reiterated in the commandments of Deuteronomy. The formula mandates the brutal expulsion of
those who violate commandments and so jeopardize
the community. (The actual wording of the formula is,
"so you shall purge . . . from your midst.") The formula
of excommunication is rendered with the verb "purge,"
to eliminate that which puts the community at risk. By
considering the use of the formula, we can see how
serious membership was taken to be and how urgent
elimination of risk was seen to be:

- purge false prophets (Deut. 13:5);
- purge murderers (17:7; 21:9);
- purge those who defy the priest (17:12);
- purge rebellious children (21:21);
- purge prostitutes (22:21);

- purge adulterers (22:22, 24);
- purge kidnappers (24:7).

The formula is used in order to justify and require acts of violent exclusion that will maintain the coherence and the safety of the community. All this data suggests the seriousness of the matter indicated by the heavy-handed measures. We may assume a level of felt threat commensurate with the extent of brutality authorized for communal maintenance.

III

This extended reflection on membership in Israel through the maintenance of purity, the practice of neighborliness, and adherence to Torah provides a milieu for the point about Sabbath-keeping that I now wish to pursue. In Isaiah 56, a text that apparently is much later than the text in Deuteronomy, the community returns to the vexed issue of membership. The text reflects the "recovery program" of Jews who had returned from Babylonian deportation and were now determined "to get it right." The community had a number of difficult issues to negotiate, as can be seen in the larger corpus of Isaiah 56–66. But no issue was more urgent than that of membership. Among the questions to be faced was the matter of admission of Jews to the worship community, those who had been deported and those who had not been deported, those who had cooperated with imperial authorities and those who had not cooperated. It is probable that Isaiah 56:3–8 reflects only one side of this urgently disputed matter, but it is the text we will consider here.

The text is one that startles us because it sets out to contradict and overthrow the ancient rules of Moses in Deuteronomy 23:1–8 by asserting a principle of *inclusiveness* against that ancient *exclusivism*. This poetic assertion advocates the option of including two groups of applicants for membership in Israel. First, welcome the *foreigners*!

Do not let the foreigner joined to the LORD say,
    "The LORD will surely separate me from his people";
. . . .
And the foreigners who join themselves to the LORD,
    to minister to him, to love the name of the LORD,
    and to be his servants,
all who keep the sabbath, and do not profane it. (Isa. 56:3a, 6)

Second, admit *eunuchs*!

And do not let the eunuch say,
    "I am just a dry tree."
. . . .
For thus says the LORD:
To the eunuchs who keep my sabbaths,
    who choose the things that please me
    and hold fast my covenant,
I will give, in my house and within my walls,
    a monument and a name
    better than sons and daughters;
I will give them an everlasting name
    that shall not be cut off. (56:3b, 4–5)

The admission of foreigners clearly contradicts the exclusion of Moabites and Ammonites in Deuteronomy 23 and seems to make it easier for Egyptians as well. It is remarkable that the advocacy of the poem is not deterred by the Torah of Moses. The stance is one of generous inclusiveness.

The admission of eunuchs, even though with different wording, would seem to be intentionally aimed at Deuteronomy 23:1, for eunuchs have "compromised" genitalia. Now it may be that the term should not be translated "eunuch," but in any case it would seem to refer to those who had cooperated with and submitted to foreign rulers and thus compromised politically, even if not with reference to genitals. But the more common translation of "eunuchs" can be taken provisionally here as reference to the latter as well. Both categories of applicants are to be made welcome; a picture is presented of a community of faith that is generously expansive and welcoming, quite unlike the initial prescription of Moses.

Most remarkably, the conditions of admission clearly do not concern ethnic qualification or any other criterion of purity. On the one hand, there is the quite generic requirement of the new recruit simply to "keep Torah." That is all. This likely means the Torah of Deuteronomy, but it is not spelled out. Most spectacularly, there is only one condition spelled out . . . keep Sabbath! This is the single, solitary mark of membership, an act of generous incorporation that outruns the inventory of Moses and that lets the life of God's Israel spill over among those who have been excluded but are now to be welcomed.

How astonishing that of all the conditions for entry into the community the party of inclusiveness might have selected, they opted for Sabbath! They made Sabbath the single specific requirement for membership. That is because Sabbath represents a radical disengagement from the producer-consumer rat race of the empire. The community welcomes members of any race or nation, any gender or social condition, so long as that person is defined by justice, mercy, and compassion, and not competition, achievement, production, or acquisition. There is no mention of purity, only work stoppage with a neighborly pause for humanness.

"These"—says the text—these foreigners, these eunuchs, these whom Moses would not admit, these Sabbath keepers, these persons of faith who refuse to be defined by cultural expectations, are to be admitted:

Thus says the LORD God,
    who gathers the outcasts of Israel,
I will gather others to them
    besides those already gathered. (Isa. 56:8)

IV

This is an ancient text that corrects an even more ancient text. And now we read this ancient text in our contemporary moment of deciding. Ours is a time of scattering in fear. We are so fearful that we want to fence the world in order to keep all the others out:

– Some of the church still wants to fence out women.
– We build fences to keep out immigrants (or Palestinians).
– The church in many places fences out gays.
– The old issue of race is still powerful for fencing.

We have so many requirements that are as old as Moses. But here is only one requirement. It is Sabbath, work stoppage, an ordinance everyone can honor—gay or straight, woman or man, Black or White, "American" or Hispanic—anybody can keep it and be gathered to the meeting of all of God's people. Sabbath deconstructs the notion of being "qualified" for membership. Later on, John the Baptist dealt with the professional insiders. They were so proud of being qualified insiders. They bragged about their pedigree, their entitlements, their ancestors, their primacy, children with family trees back to Father Abraham. And John scolds them and rejects their pedigree:

> Do not presume to say to yourselves, "We have Abraham as our ancestor"; for I tell you, God is able from these stones to raise up children to Abraham. (Matt. 3:9)

And then he says that what counts is not pedigree, what counts is fruit:

> Even now the ax is lying at the root of the trees; every tree therefore that does not bear good fruit is cut down and thrown into the fire. (3:10)

What counts are the outcomes of your life.

I pondered the word "fruit" . . . outcome. And I remembered Paul on fruit. He said of bad fruit:

> Now the works of the flesh are obvious: fornication, impurity, licentiousness, idolatry, sorcery, enmities, strife, jealousy, anger, quarrels, dissensions, factions, envy, drunkenness, carousing, and things like these. I am warning you, as I warned you before: those who do such things will not inherit the kingdom of God. (Gal. 5:19–21)

But then he celebrated the alternative:

> By contrast, the fruit of the Spirit is love, joy, peace, patience, kindness, generosity, faithfulness, gentleness, and self-control. There is no law against such things. (5:22–23)

I dare to think that the "good fruits" arise from the "peaceableness" of Sabbath. The "destructive fruits" of the flesh are generated by rat-race living. The advocates in Isaiah 56 want no rat-race companions. They want, rather, the fruits that arise from work stoppage. And then it occurred to me. With reference to "fruit," we have come full circle from where we began these explorations. It was at the beginning that God blessed the human creatures and said to them, "Be fruitful." The God who gave the blessing and invited fruitfulness is the Lord of the Sabbath. It requires Sabbath to bear the fruits of God's kingdom. Those who refuse Sabbath produce only sour grapes, the grapes of wrath and violence and envy and, finally, death. Sabbath is a refusal of the grapes of wrath, an embrace of good fruits of life and joy, of praise and *shalom*.

Chapter 5

RESISTANCE
TO MULTITASKING

Amos 8:4–8

WHEN I WAS GROWING UP IN RURAL SALINE COUNTY, Missouri, "Mr. G.," our town grocer, and his wife always sat up front in church. Every Sunday, during the last five minutes of the sermon by the pastor (my father), Mr. G. and his wife would rather ceremoniously walk the long aisle to the back of the church and leave. They did not mind the distraction of their maneuver to everyone else at worship. The reason they left is that the other church in town, the Missouri Synod Lutheran Church, got out of service thirty minutes earlier than we "E & R" Christians finished worship. As a kid, I often wondered how often Mr. G. had looked at his watch during the service to be sure he left on time to receive Lutheran trade and Lutheran money. I did not know the phrase at the time, but Mr. G. was "multitasking." He was worshiping, even while he kept an eye on the clock for the sake of trade and profit. I will, in a moment, return to the issue of multitasking.

I

In this exposition, I will consider prophetic critique in the Old Testament of Israel's compromised, inadequate ways of keeping Sabbath. As Moses had anticipated in the book of Deuteronomy, Israel was seduced in the land, seduced to forgetting the exodus God and thinking they could secure themselves. I call this "the turn to commodity," to the conviction that having more would generate well-being. The lead representative figure in the turn of ancient Israel to commodity is Solomon, as offered in the book of Kings:

– Solomon's grandiose temple was a commodity enterprise, marked by endless amounts of gold, surely designed to impress:

> The interior of the inner sanctuary was twenty cubits long, twenty cubits wide, and twenty cubits high; he overlaid it with pure gold. He also overlaid the altar with cedar. Solomon overlaid the inside of the house with pure gold, then he drew chains of gold across, in front of the inner sanctuary, and overlaid it with gold. . . .
>
> So Solomon made all the vessels that were in the house of the LORD: the golden altar, the golden table for the bread of the Presence, the lampstands of pure gold, five on the south side and five on the north, in front of the inner sanctuary; the flowers, the lamps, and the tongs, of gold; the cups, snuffers, basins, dishes for incense, and firepans, of pure gold; the sockets for the doors of the nave of the temple, of gold. (1 Kgs. 6:20–21; 7:48–50)

– Beyond the temple, Solomon was the big time entrepreneur who managed to amass every kind of commodity imaginable. And like all such celebrity accumulators, others were eager to contribute to Solomon's collection:

> Every one of them brought a present, objects of silver and gold, garments, weaponry, spices, horses, and mules, so much year by year. (10:25)

– In addition to temple gold and exotic possessions, Solomon's accumulation of women points to the conclusion that even women—wives and concubines—had become commodities for the king, either trophy mates or instruments of policy (11:3).

This threefold acquisitiveness testifies to a kind of restlessness on Solomon's part. It is easiest to imagine that Solomon never ceased to plan and scheme and negotiate and usurp in his drive to accumulate. Such restlessness in the service of acquisitiveness surely meant no Sabbath for him. We may judge, moreover, that Solomon is a representative embodiment of commodity restlessness that pervaded Israel in its disregard for all things covenantal.

II

In the Old Testament, the prophets in their various modes of rhetoric consistently voice a critique of the turn to commodity and issue a summons to return to covenantal ways for which the restfulness of Sabbath may be taken as a sign and measure. The restfulness of Sabbath is an act of resistance to commodity acquisition. But in acquisitive Israel, so well represented by Solomon, Sabbath became a fake occasion, an official act of work stoppage; it was in fact a festival shot through with anxiety and aggressiveness fed by commodity acquisitiveness with which Israel had become enthralled. I will cite three prophetic references and then focus on one poem in the tradition of Amos that exposes the multitasking of distorted Sabbath as a fraud.

– *Isaiah 1:12–17.* This prophetic oracle is divided into two parts. In verses 12–15 the poem declares YHWH's disappointment and exhaustion with Israel's worship that is vigorous but repulsive to YHWH. Indeed YHWH "hates" their worship, is "weary" of their festivals that are a "burden," and resolves not to listen to their prayers. The indictment includes a full inventory of liturgical practices: offerings, incense, new moons, convocations, solemn assemblies, and prayers. Included in this catalogue, not surprisingly, is Sabbath, one of the assemblies done "with iniquity." These lines do not tell us what is wrong with Israel's worship.

In the second part of the oracle (vv. 16–17), however, we learn of the problem. The prophet issues a series of imperatives to Israel concerning its failed worship. These imperatives include a call to ritual purification, but they build toward a rhetorical climax with justice for the oppressed, the orphans, and the widows. These urgent requirements indicate the problem with Israel's worship. Its liturgical activity is cut off from the well-being of the neighborhood and the protection of the vulnerable, that is, removed from covenantal modes of reality. This suggests that worshipers in Israel, in the keeping of Sabbath, had not desisted from acquisitiveness that inevitably caused exploitation of the unprotected. They may have gone through the motions of Sabbath, but they did not stop the practices of anxiety, coercion, and exploitation that real work stoppage would entail. Their acquisitive enterprise had such momentum that it carried right into and through the Sabbath. The great festival of rest had become simply another venue for restlessness.

– *Hosea 2:8–13.* In this prophetic indictment, cast as a divorce proceeding, YHWH speaks as an aggrieved husband who is offended by the conduct of wife-Israel. (The sexist perspective of the text has been often noted and is here acknowledged.) Israel's affront against YHWH the creator is that it did not recognize that YHWH, the creator, is the one "who gave her the grain, the wine, and the oil" (v. 8). That is, Israel did not acknowledge YHWH as generous creator but assumed that Baal, the Canaanite god, was the sustainer of creation.

YHWH's angry retaliation against Israel is to "take back" grain and wine, to "take away" wool and flax, that is, to shut down creation (v. 9). Verses 10–13 feature a series of YHWH's resolves in first-person verbs:

- I will put an end.
- I will lay waste.
- I will make a forest.
- I will punish.

YHWH will shut down Israel's life as creation is to be shut down. The ultimate reason for the shutdown, as Moses had anticipated, is that Israel "forgot me" (v. 13).

What interests us is verse 11:

I will put an end to all her mirth,
  her festivals, her new moons, her sabbaths,
  and all her appointed festivals.

As in Isaiah 1, there is a recital of worship festivals, including new moons and Sabbaths. The indictment is that Israel had celebrated Sabbath, all the while multitasking, going through the motions of YHWH worship but in fact trusting in and honoring Baal, the Canaanite god of generativity, who had no interest in covenantal obligations or covenantal possibilities. Due to such doublemindedness, Sabbath lacked authenticity and in fact did not entail a genuine work stoppage from the restless anxiety that comes with anticovenantal existence. Such inauthentic Sabbath provides no rest and leads to a fundamental alienation from God and from neighbor.

— *Isaiah 58:1–7.* In this much later text, the prophet reflects on a dispute about correct worship. In an easy and overly obvious contrast, the poem sets in juxtaposition two models of worship, both of which are called "fasts." On the one hand, there is ritual fasting among those who "delight" to draw near to God, that is, to come to church (v. 2). But while going through the motions of worship, fast, and humbleness (v. 3), in fact the Israelite worshipers practice exploitative economics and oppress their workers. While Sabbath is not explicitly mentioned, it is clear that the worship under consideration did not allow for sabbatical work stoppage. There is in this practice no justice for or generosity toward workers. This worship contradicts neighborliness and provides a cover of legitimacy for exploitation.

On the other hand, by contrast, the poem proposes an authentic "fast" that includes justice toward the oppressed, bread for the hungry, housing for the poor, clothing for the naked, that is, genuine neighborly covenantal support. This worship is congruent with the Deuteronomic commands concerning the vulnerable in society.

Now it may be that this text does not belong directly to a discussion of Sabbath. The issue is posed more broadly about worship and neighborliness. But since Sabbath is the quintessential worship act of neighborliness wherein the workers rest "as you" (Deut. 5:14), we may see in this context a contrast with a practice of worship that offers no Sabbath rest but only reflects a social restlessness and feeds social restlessness by giving it religious legitimacy. Worship that does not lead to neighborly compassion and justice cannot be faithful worship of YHWH. The offer is a phony Sabbath!

III

The critiques of Isaiah 1:12–17, Hosea 2:8–13, and Isaiah 58:1–7 prepare us for the fuller, more direct oracle of Amos. Amos is well known for his social critique. He exposes the limitless consumerism and pursuit of commodity by his well-known indictment of acquisitive wives:

> Hear this word, you cows of Bashan
>   who are on Mount Samaria,
> who oppress the poor, who crush the needy,
>   who say to their husbands, "Bring something to
>   drink!" (Amos 4:1)

He offers an almost pornographic description of the endless self-indulgence among the privileged in their entitlement:

> Alas for those who lie on beds of ivory,
>   and lounge on their couches,
> and eat lambs from the flock,
>   and calves from the stall;
> who sing idle songs to the sound of the harp,
>   and like David improvise on instruments of music;
> who drink wine from bowls,
>   and anoint themselves with the finest oils. (6:4-6a)

He catalogs their idle entertainment that includes the consumption of lambs and calves, while peasants would not dare to slaughter animals so young. The self-indulgence is reported as lounging in exotic (ivory) furnishings with trivial music, enormous amounts of alcohol, splendid cosmetics of every kind. That inventory of commodity commitment ends with a powerful adversative "but" in verse 6:

> but are not grieved over the ruin of Joseph! (6:6b)

Amos describes those who are so numbed that they do not notice the extravagance of life based on cheap labor that sooner or later will evoke social crisis.

The "therefore" of verse 7 is an ominous poetic conclusion to this scathing indictment. Such self-congratulatory numbness, says the poet, will inescapably lead to social demise. Only the entitled are so narcotized that they are unable to see trouble coming.

The indictment of acquisitiveness (4:1) and of numbness (6:4-7) prepares us for the stunning oracle on Sabbath in Amos 8:4–8. The indictment in verses 4–6 is simply a description of what happens in an acquisitive society among his contemporaries. The oracle begins with a declaration that the economy operates to "trample, ruin" the poor and needy (v. 4). But the ones who do the exploitation do not notice; they are at worship! They are keeping Sabbath! They are honoring their religious mores . . . all the time watching the clock. They can hardly bear to keep Sabbath and cannot wait until Sabbath is finally over at sundown, in order to rush to resume commerce:

> saying, "When will the new moon be over
>   so that we may sell grain;
> and the sabbath,
>   so that we may offer wheat for sale?
> We will make the ephah small and the shekel great,
>   and practice deceit with false balances." (8:5)

All the while they keep Sabbath, they are in fact, in their imaginations, buying and selling and trading and bargaining. The appearance is one of *rest*, but, says the poet, the social reality is one of *restlessness*, for the pattern of acquisitiveness is not interrupted, even on the day of rest.

But more than that, the eagerness to return to commerce is not only to engage in economic activity. Verse 5 states that much:

> . . . so that we may offer wheat for sale.

The next lines concern eagerness not only for trade but for distorted, dishonest trade, using dishonest scales (on which see the prohibition in Deut. 25:13–16). The inevitable consequence of such rigged measures is that the poor—who do not know any better or who do not pay attention—are the ones who finance the distorted market. In the end the poor are made into a tradable commodity (v. 6). They are reduced to an equivalency for a pair of shoes or a silver coin. Everything has become a commodity; and there are no more neighbors!

But more, says Amos. If performed Sabbath does not in reality break the pattern of restless acquisitiveness, trouble will come. A society that refuses Sabbath restfulness for all is bound to fail, says the prophet:

The land will tremble . . . and mourn. (8:8)

On that day . . . mourning . . . lamentations . . . sackcloth . . . baldness. (vv. 9–10)

The time is surely coming . . . .famine . . . of the word. (vv. 11–12)

IV

They keep Sabbath, all the while scheming for commodities. This is an epitome of "multitasking." In my horizon, the most unwelcome form of multitasking is with the cell phone—on the phone while at dinner with a guest or while driving. But a much more poisonous form of multitasking is taking notes during a church service . . . not notes on the sermon but a grocery list or calls to return or deals to make. Multitasking is the drive to be more than we are, to control more than we do, to extend our power and our effectiveness. Such practice yields a divided self, with full attention given to nothing.

Jesus offers an ominous characterization of "multi-tasking" with which Amos would have resonated:

> No one can serve two masters; for a slave will either hate the one and love the other, or be devoted to the one and despise the other. You cannot serve God and wealth. (Matt. 6:24)

To serve *God* and *wealth* at the same time is impossible. It is like keeping Sabbath and at the same time planning for commerce. It is like making deep love but all the while watching the clock. It is like praising Jesus while preying on the poor. Such multitasking with a divided heart means that there is no real work stoppage, no interruption in the frantic attempt to get ahead. Doing tasks of acquisitiveness while trying to communicate humanly is the true mark of the "turn to commodity." We all become commodities to one another, to be bought and sold and traded and cheated.

There is no doubt that "Mr. G." back in Saline County was multitasking. He had to watch the clock while at worship so as not to miss out on Lutheran customers. It is probable, however, that "Mr. G." is not unlike most of us. We have made "the turn to commodity." The Sabbath command is an urgent summons to break the pattern of the divided heart . . . before it is too late. No wonder Jesus followed Matthew 6:24 with verse 25:

"Do not be anxious!"

Chapter 6

SABBATH AND THE TENTH COMMANDMENT

THE FOURTH COMMANDMENT ON SABBATH COMPELS REST for all members of the household, all members of the community, human and animal. As such it looks forward to the last six commandments that concern neighborly relations (Exod. 20:12–17). The fourth commandment anticipates a peaceable household and neighborhood and sets out a discipline and limit that will serve that peaceableness. The six commandments that follow on neighborliness reach a climactic point in the tenth commandment on coveting that is presented, perhaps, as the act that is the ultimate destruction of the neighborhood, for coveting generates mistrust and sets neighbor against neighbor.

That tenth commandment has very often been distinguished from the preceding commandments by suggesting that unlike the others, it concerns only an intent or an attitude and not an act, thus unlike forcible actions of "killing, committing adultery, or stealing." But that is almost surely a mistaken interpretation of the commandment. Coveting is understood, in biblical tradition, as including both an *attitude of craving* and *forceful action* to secure what is craved. It underscores the force of lustful desire but knows that the danger to the community comes when the craving is acted on. Thus, the commandment concerns a *posture* and *practice* of acquisitiveness, the capacity and readiness to acquire what properly belongs to another and so to place the well-being of the other in jeopardy.

The specifics of such community-destroying greed include "house and wife." "House" refers to the entire socioeconomic aggregate of a village household. In a patriarchal society, moreover, a wife may be reckoned as a principal "property" along with the "house," not as an object, but as one who "belongs to" and "belongs with" the male head of the household. Beyond "house and wife," the prohibition concerns the householder's "means of production," that is, economic viability: slaves, ox, and donkey. It is prohibited to infringe economically on the well-being of others. After the prohibition of these named objects—house, wife, means of production—the commandment ends with a conclusion so sweeping that nothing is exempt from the rule: "everything that belongs to your neighbor."

What strikes one about this list is that in a very brief statement of prohibition the term "neighbor" occurs three times. It is all about respecting the neighbor, and so it is all about preserving, honoring, and enhancing the neighborhood. It is most probable that the neighborhood in purview was an agrarian village of vulnerable peasants, each of whom lived a vulnerable economic existence with no margin for loss. For that reason, any disturbance of property arrangements had the potential of making life in the village unlivable. Thus Sabbath rest in context means to protect the space and property of the neighbor from the restlessness that disrupts and skews social relationships by desisting from acquisitive practices. There is no doubt that the Torah, most particularly in the tradition of Deuteronomy, is concerned for neighbors, and especially the most vulnerable of neighbors: widows, orphans, and immigrants. These are the ones who are most vulnerable to economic interference through which they may be reduced to helplessness, poverty, and a lack of viability. The commandment thus seems to be a quite particular rule concerning the love of neighbor, which Jesus subsequently identified as the "second great commandment" (Mark 12:28–34). The neighbor is to be loved as self, and the property of the neighbor—his house, wife, means of production— are to be protected even as one wants one's own house, wife, and means of production left undisturbed.

As we have seen with the term "Egypt" in the first commandment, so the terms "house, wife, means of production" in the tenth commandment plunge us into socioeconomic concerns in which covenantal prohibition forbids the kind of economic free-for-all that might favor the rich and powerful against the poor and vulnerable. In context, moreover, this way of plotting the dynamics of social-economic power likely reflects a recurring practice in that ancient world. These were agrarian peasants at the mercy of urban elites who are backed by and in solidarity with the power of the centralized city-state, the legitimacy of centralized temple worship, and the effective expertise of the scribal-legal guild. If this social plot is described correctly as an uneven contest between *agrarian peasants* and *urban elites*, then one may imagine how vulnerable the rural peasants were with their small farms in the face of such coercive urban capacity. In contemporary analogue, we might imagine the allied force of *the state* with its management of the economy by those who control the levers of government, *corporate wealth* and influence, *legal sharpness*, and the legitimating power of *credentialed religion*. In the face of such unequal power arrangements, the prohibition of the tenth commandment draws a line of protection, which recognizes that such acquisitive power does indeed exist, but it must be curbed in the interest of the common good.

It is most likely that the "law of release" in Deuteronomy 15:1–18 reflects the reality of such unequal social power. In this provision, Moses summons Israel, surely the creditor class, to cancel debts on the poor and vulnerable at the end of seven years, in order that there should be no permanent underclass, and to subordinate the economy to the common good. The sharp warning issued by Moses that the creditors should not be "hard-hearted" or "tight fisted" indicates an ideological resistance to such a covenantal requirement and limitation (v. 8). Thus, the provision in Deuteronomy 15 is a counterpoint to the prohibition of the tenth commandment, both of which mean to curb the devouring power of entrenched economic force aimed against the vulnerable. We may cite a number of biblical texts that will serve to exposit the tenth commandment.

— *1 Kings 21:1–29.* The narrative account of the seizure of the property of Naboth by King Ahab and Queen Jezebel in 1 Kings 21 is paradigmatic for our commandment. The narrative is situated in the cycle of Elijah accounts so that we may anticipate that it has a critical perspective against entrenched royal power. Though the term "covet" is not used in the narrative, it well exposits the commandment. The drama reflects the map of socioeconomic power in that ancient world. Naboth is a small-time farmer whose land is his "ancestral inheritance." It belongs to his family even as he himself belongs to the land. The relationship of person and land is close and beyond question.

The royal enterprise, by contrast, is fully emancipated from such "ancestral" notions of property and views all property as a tradable commodity. Thus Ahab and Jezebel are an embodiment of an acquisitive worldview before which traditional claims are weak and malleable. Naboth resists the royal initiative only by reiterating his claim. But the royal couple, completely impervious to such claims, will stop at nothing until they are able to "take possession" of his ancestral heritage. This narrative makes clear that "coveting" is not only a desire for but also the active capacity to seize what one desires. It is no wonder the narrative clash of economic systems evokes the ominous entry of Elijah, whose presence and words contradict the acquisitive effort of the royal party that he judges to be unsustainable (vv. 17–24).

— Micah 2:1–5. The oracle of Micah 2:1–5 more explicitly comments on "coveting." Micah is a spokesperson for the small agrarian peasants who engage, as they are able, in resistance against the urban elites in Jerusalem (see Jer. 26:17–18). This oracle is organized around an initial "alas" ("woe") that anticipates deathly trouble (Mic. 2:2), a "therefore" of consequence (v. 3), and a climactic "therefore" (v. 5). The indictment in verses 1–2 speaks of plotting at night ("on their beds") and performing the plot in the day ("morning dawns"). The two time slots, night and day, bespeak the *power of desire* and the *power to secure* what one desires. The plot and the performance of it are about coveting, seizing, taking away, and oppression. It is all about confiscation! And the object of such coercive desire is "fields," "houses," "people," and "inheritance." The terms are parallel to the theme of the Naboth narrative.

The first two verses portray an economic enterprise in which the "wicked" are the rapacious urban land speculators who exploit the vulnerability of the peasants. We might think of the usurpers as urban developers who exercise the right of eminent domain or bankers who foreclose on failed loans, or government or church officials who know a prize location when they see it. Indeed, the poetry concerns the entire system that runs roughshod over the claims of "inheritance." The initial "alas" voices the prophetic conviction that such confiscation in order to develop larger estates is a lethal, unsustainable enterprise.

The "therefore" that follows introduces a poetic sketch of the "I" of YHWH, the guarantor of old ancestral inheritances who will "devise" evil against the coveters as they have "devised" in the first place. The "devising of evil" by YHWH (in response to their "devising of evil") will result in "an evil time to come." It will be a time of utter ruin when the "inheritance" of my "people" (not just the little inheritances of the peasants) will be in shambles. The poetry, in context, anticipates the coming of the Assyrian armies before which the urban elites in Jerusalem will be helpless. Thus the poetry connects observable *coveting practices* and anticipated *external imperial threat.* The connection of the one to the other is the work of the governance of YHWH. The outcome will be that the self-aggrandizement of the coveters will be reduced to "bitter lamentation" (v. 4).

The speculators now will watch helplessly as the invaders redistribute the land away from their aggressiveness. The final verse 5, introduced by yet another "therefore," anticipates that when the meeting is held by the empire to reassign the land, the wicked speculators will not be admitted to the meeting. They will get nothing! The poem enacts a radical social inversion evoked by YHWH. The outcome is a repudiation of the policies of the coveters. For that reason, as the commandment enjoins, "Thou shalt not!"
— *Isaiah 5:8–10.* The oracle in Micah has a close parallel in the poetic oracle of Isaiah 5:8–10. This poetic segment also begins with "Ah" ("woe"), anticipating big trouble to come because of destructive social behavior. The indictment is against those who "join house to house" and "field to field," exactly the language of the commandment and of the Micah oracle. The process consists of buying up the land of small

peasant farmers in order to develop large estates. The vulnerable peasants are then removed from their land and denied a livelihood, and now coveters can bask in their newly secured isolated self-indulgence. The prophetic judgment pertains to such rural displacement; in our time, the same crisis might refer to urban gentrification that dislocates the poor and the vulnerable. The poetry traces the destruction, by acquisitiveness, of a viable neighborly infrastructure.

The introduction of the "LORD of Hosts" in verse 9 indicates that such a rapacious economic transaction does not go unnoticed. The inescapable outcome of such land dealing, in the perspective of YHWH, is that such extravagances are unsustainable. In ways beyond explanation, the poetry declares a great reversal to come of what is both unsustainable and unacceptable so that many "large and beautiful houses" will be destroyed and abandoned. Worse than that, the agricultural land that is no longer cared for by attentive peasants will simply fail to produce. One might imagine that such a prospect about loss of productivity constitutes an early warning concerning agribusiness that will eventually ruin the land by neglect. The prophetic oracle is, in sum, an exposition of the tenth commandment. The reason "thou shalt not" is that neither the human community nor the land can tolerate such abusive policies long term.

— *Deuteronomy 19:14; Proverbs 22:28 and 23:10–11.* The old "ancestral inheritances" were sustained by long, fixed boundary lines, likely with fences and post markers, that were taken as abiding givens. But the coveters chose, in principle, to disregard such old markers in the interest of greater profits. They no doubt did so with legal protections enacted by their elitist government. But the old "ancestral inheritances" would not yield so easily because that tradition understood that violation of such boundaries would upend and disrupt the entire casting of social relationships. Thus in both Torah and wisdom tradition, the moving of such boundary markers was prohibited, as a subset of the tenth commandment:

> You must not move your neighbor's boundary marker, set up by former generations, on the property that will be allotted to you in the land that the LORD your God is giving you to possess. (Deut. 19:14)

> Do not remove the ancient landmark
> that your ancestors set up. (Prov. 22:28)

> Do not remove an ancient landmark
> or encroach on the fields of orphans,
> for their redeemer is strong;
> he will plead their cause against you. (Prov. 23:10–11)

The tenth commandment is a safeguard for a certain way of organizing social power in the interest of the neighborhood. Such neighborliness is eroded and eventually destroyed when the unchecked acquisitiveness of the powerful preys on the vulnerable.
— *Jeremiah 5:22; 5:26–28; 6:13, 14; 30:12, 15; and 8:10–12.* As the prophetic tradition moves closer to the culminating crisis of the destruction of Jerusalem, the poetic rhetoric of the prophetic tradition becomes more intense. The social analysis of Jeremiah voices the crisis of inequity between "scoundrels" (5:26) who are "great and rich . . . fat and sleek" who operate with treachery

against "the orphan" and "the needy" who are defenseless (vv. 27–28). This sketch of social power concerns the force of an acquisitive economy in which the powerful want and take what the vulnerable have. These practices transgress the "boundaries" of the creator who provides a safe place for the life of all (v. 22). The "scoundrels" have crossed over these boundaries in their rapacious practices (v. 28). The tenth commandment is an effort to set a limit on such systemic greediness, but Jerusalem now hosts an economy in which such boundaries have collapsed. The outcome is an economic free-for-all with the "rights of the needy" completely disregarded.

Thus Jeremiah draws a concluding judgment on the transgressors:

> From the least to the greatest of them,
>   everyone is greedy for unjust gain;
> and from prophet to priest,
>   everyone deals falsely. (6:13)

The phrase "greedy for unjust gain" does not employ the wording of the tenth commandment. But the intent is the same. All have become predators and coveters. All have skewed social relationships by dealing falsely. The urban leadership—"from priest to prophet"—all have disregarded the prohibition of the tenth commandment.

In order to make such an acquisitive economy work, it is necessary to disguise the true economy with the euphemisms of well-being that contradict the facts on the ground:

> They have treated the wound of my people carelessly,
>   Saying, "Peace, peace,"
> when there is no peace. (v. 14)

The wound in the body politic is acute, later on in 30:12 said to be incurable. But the wound is perforce denied by the use of political slogans and popular mantras. The ideology of exceptionalism in Jeru*salem*, a city named for *shalom*, will override all such social suffering. Thus under the banner of ideology, the practices of exploitative acquisitive economy go unchecked. They remain unchecked, says the poet, except for the divine "therefore" of verse 15. In the meantime, an acquisitiveness that despises and degrades the vulnerable in its greed becomes shameless:

> They acted shamefully, they committed abomination;
>   yet they were not ashamed,
>   they did not know how to blush.
> Therefore . . . (v. 15)

This prophetic exposition of the tenth commandment is reiterated in 8:10–12, a repetition that suggests it has become a tag-word for the advocates of the old social relationships that are to be restored. All these Old Testament texts attest to restless assertive cynicism in a community that is completely unaware of its own self-destructiveness, except for the few who remain grounded in the old covenantal traditions.

— *Luke 12:13–34.* The tenth commandment of course runs, in Christian tradition, toward the teaching of Jesus. In the parable of Luke 12:13–34, Jesus summarizes the "two ways" that are as old as covenant and as poignant as the Naboth narrative. In response to the man in dispute with his brother over the family inheritance (!), Jesus provides the pivot point of his instruction:

> Take care! Be on your guard against all kinds of
> greed; for one's life does not consist in the abundance
> of possessions. (12:15)

This statement is a near parallel to the tenth commandment. In the NRSV it is "greed"; in earlier rendering, it is "covetousness." What follows is a scenario
of the coveting man who, like the "wicked" in Micah
2, the land speculators in Isaiah 5, and the "scoundrels" in Jeremiah 5, devours the land and the houses
of the vulnerable. The greedy man in the parable is a
huge success in his own eyes; but, contrary to his own
estimate, he is destined for death in his self-deceiving
foolishness.

From his act of narrative imagination, Jesus draws
instruction for his disciples: Do not be anxious (v. 22)!
Do not worry about commodity goods. It is implied
that an acquisitive way of life leaves one in anxiety
about not yet (ever!) having enough and always need-
ing more. Thus discipleship, in this teaching, concerns
a life alternative to acquisitiveness. That alternative
is grounded in confidence that God provides what is
needed, as energy is redeployed to "strive for his kingdom" (v. 31). Jesus invites to alternative, even as the
Sinai commandment hosts an alternative of covenantal
neighborliness.

It turns out that the implications of the tenth commandment were important in the recurring teaching of
the apostolic church. It may be that such teaching was
conventional and stylized. It is nonetheless remarkable
that the import of the tenth commandment is at the
center of such teaching. Early Christians were attentive to the ideology of acquisitiveness and the compul-

sive power of greed. We may notice five such instances from the early epistles of the church:

1. *Paul includes the tenth commandment in his summary that culminates with the neighbor:*

> The commandments, "You shall not commit adultery; You shall not murder; You shall not steal; You shall not covet"; and any other commandment, are summed up in this word, "Love your neighbor as yourself." (Rom. 13:9)

Love of neighbor is alternative to acquisitiveness (see 1:29; 7:7)!

2. *In Ephesians 5:3–5, greed is twice listed among the distractions to be avoided:*

> But fornication and impurity of any kind, or greed, must not even be mentioned among you, as is proper among saints. Entirely out of place is obscene, silly, and vulgar talk, but instead, let there be thanksgiving. Be sure of this, that no fornicator, or impure person, or anyone who is greedy (that is, an idolater) has any inheritance in the kingdom of Christ and of God. (5:3–5)

The counter to such destructive conduct is thanksgiving! Such a teaching may suggest echoes of Luke 12. Acquisitiveness, among other vices, is the antithesis of thanksgiving, one based in possessions, the other in gifts.

3. *In the parallel passage of Colossians 3, the point is the same:*

> Put to death, therefore, whatever in you is earthly: fornication, impurity, passion, evil desire, and greed (which is idolatry). (v. 5)

The list, taken in sum, amounts to the "old self." The writer knows that this cluster of practices always comes together; they are rooted in a sense of self that is immune to the truth of neighborliness. By contrast, the focus on neighborliness constitutes an embrace of a new life with a new set of practices:

> [Y]ou have stripped off the old self with its practices and have clothed yourselves with the new self, which is being renewed in knowledge according to the image of its creator. (vv. 9–10)

The new self is situated in the midst of the neighbors, and new conduct is grounded in neighbor-regard:

> As God's chosen ones, holy and beloved, clothe yourselves with compassion, kindness, humility, meekness, and patience. Bear with one another and, if anyone has a complaint against another, forgive each other. (vv. 12–13)

One will not fail to notice that the term "forgive" occurs twice, perhaps the pivot point of the new life. If such forgiveness includes "the forgiveness of debts," it may include a contradiction of all acquisitiveness that thrives on indebtedness. The vision of an alternative is central to the life of the emerging church, even when its mandates are as old as Sinai.

4. *James reflects on the disputes in the church grounded in "cravings":*

> Those conflicts and disputes among you, where do they come from? Do they not come from your cravings that are at war within you? You want something and do not have it; so you commit murder. And you

covet something and cannot obtain it; so you engage in disputes and conflicts. You do not have it, because you do not ask. (4:1–2)

"Cravings" create conflict and dispute and disrupt the neighborhood. The accent on "asking" in verse 2 suggests an alternative to craving that is a transaction of gift, of asking and receiving.

5. *Second Peter 2 voices a harangue against false prophets.* Among the many indictments of them is this passionate characterization:

> They have eyes full of adultery, insatiable for sin. They entice unsteady souls. They have hearts trained in greed. Accursed children! (v. 14)

The rhetoric of "adultery . . . insatiable . . . entice" suggests a notion that all of life is an object of conquest and exploitation. To be "trained in greed" means to reduce all of life to a tradable commodity. Clearly, the point of this diatribe is to urge and warn the church that it is to be otherwise engaged in a different set of practices:

> For this very reason, you must make every effort to support your faith with goodness, and goodness with knowledge, and knowledge with self-control, and self-control with endurance, and endurance with godliness, and godliness with mutual affection, and mutual affection with love. For if these things are yours and are increasing among you, they keep you from being ineffective and unfruitful in the knowledge of our Lord Jesus Christ. (1:5–8)

This accumulated testimony from the earliest church leaves for us the task of drawing an obvious conclusion. Ours, like that ancient society of Israel and like the context of the early church, offers a social script for a social system of coveting acquisitiveness. Indeed, our consumer society is grounded in the generation of artificial desires, readily transposed into urgent needs. The always-emerging new desires and new needs create a restless striving that sets neighbor against neighbor in order to get ahead, to have an advantage, and to accumulate at the expense of the other. The power of such a compulsion to "get," of course, negates neighborly possibility.

Beyond one-to-one transactions, this capacity for acquisitiveness is front and center in our public life and in the formation of public policy. We are able to watch while adherence to the common good disappears into a rhetoric of "opportunity" that simply means to deregulate society so predatory acts by those with leverage and will to do so go unchecked.

When coveting is systemic as it is among us, one must ask about restraint and resistance to such policy formation and social practice. Such restraint takes the form of regulation, and it is possible to see that the tenth commandment is exactly such an act of "regulation" in the community of covenant-imposed restraint. But such regulation becomes exceedingly difficult when the ideology of greed permeates the very fabric of common life. There is, in such an environment, little will for such restraint.

We are left, I suggest, with the question of how to break the lethal cycle of acquisitiveness. And so, in the context of our more general discussion, I wish to situate the tenth commandment in the context of the fourth commandment on Sabbath. Sabbath is the practical ground for breaking the power of acquisitiveness and for creating a public will for an accent on restraint. Sabbath is the cessation of widely shared practices of acquisitiveness. It provides time, space, energy, and imagination for coming to the ultimate recognition that more commodities, which may be acquired in the rough and ready of daily economics, finally do not satisfy. Sabbath is variously restraint, withdrawal, or divestment from the concrete practices of society that specialize in anxiety. Sabbath is an antidote to anxiety that both derives from our craving and in turn feeds those cravings for more. Sabbath is an arena in which to recognize that we live by gift and not by possession, that we are satisfied by relationships of attentive fidelity and not by amassing commodities. We know in the gospel tradition that we may indeed "gain the whole world" and lose our souls (Mark 8:34–37). Thus Sabbath is soul-receiving when we are in a posture of receptivity before our Father who knows we need them (Luke 12:30).

At the end of our reflection, we may consider the way in which the Sabbath commandment occupies the pivotal place in the sum of the commandments. At the outset, we discerned that the Sabbath commandment looks back to the emancipating God of the exodus who delivered from the restless productivity of Pharaoh and who rests on the seventh day. We observed that the Sabbath commandment looks forward to a possible neighborliness in which striving for commodities in community-destroying ways is prohibited. Thus the fourth commandment reaches back to commandment one and forward to commandment ten. The two commands, one and ten, come together in startling interpretation, no doubt in the wake of rabbinic awareness (emphasis added):

> Be sure of this, that no fornicator or impure person, or one who is *greedy* (that is, an *idolater*) has any inheritance in the kingdom of Christ and of God. (Eph. 5:5)

> Put to death, therefore, whatever in you is earthly: fornication, impurity, passion, evil desire, and *greed* which is *idolatry*). (Col. 3:5)

Almost incidentally and without calling attention to it, these testimonies identify *idolatry* that is rejected in commandment one and *greed* that is rejected in commandment 10. The two, idolatry and greed, are equated because both of them reduce livable reality to commodity. Idolatry is the worship (overvaluing) of things, especially things cast in gold and silver:

> A tree from the forest is cut down,
>   and worked with an ax by the hands of an artisan;
> people deck it with silver and gold;
>   they fasten it with hammer and nails
>   so that it cannot move.
> Their idols are like scarecrows in a cucumber field,
>   and they cannot speak;
> they have to be carried,
>   for they cannot walk.
> Do not be afraid of them,
>   for they cannot do evil,
>   nor is it in them to do good. (Jer. 10:3–5)

Coveting, at the other end of the Decalogue, consists in the pursuit of commodity at the expense of the neighbor.

Sabbath is a big no for both; it is no to the worship of commodity; it is no to the pursuit of commodity. But it is more than no. Sabbath is the regular, disciplined, visible, concrete yes to the neighborly reality of the community beloved by God. We used to sing the hymn "Take Time to Be Holy." But perhaps we should be singing, "Take time to be human." Or finally, "Take time." Sabbath is taking time . . . time to be holy . . . time to be human.

Psalm 73, my final text, is a report on a journey from the world of commodity to the world of communion. In verses 2–16, the psalmist ruminates over the seduction of the "wicked." The "wicked" are

- prosperous (v. 3),
- "not in trouble" (v. 5),
- proud (v. 6),
- well-fed and well-entertained (v. 7),
- cynical and socially indifferent (v. 8),
- treated like celebrities (v. 10),
- defiant before and dismissive of God (v. 11), and
- rich and "at ease" (v. 12).

Not bad! So says the psalmist; he is much attracted to such a life and thinks to enlist in it, until . . . until he reflects (v. 15) . . . until he goes to the sanctuary (v. 17) . . . until he comes to know that such a way in the world has no staying power (vv. 18–19) . . . until he discerns that he himself was simply obdurate (vv. 21–22).

And then the psalmist utters his big "nevertheless" (that in Hebrew is only a conjunction) with an emphatic pronoun (v. 23). Now everything is changed and differently perceived. Now the psalmist asks a different question:

> Whom have I in heaven but you? (v. 25a)

Answer: No one! I have no other! The parallel line is not a question, but a verdict of settled reality:

> And there is nothing on earth that I desire other
> than you. (v. 25b)

It is, the psalmist recognizes, a question of "desire" (*hps*). The psalmist comes to an acute awareness of the true desire of his life; he discovers in that moment that the life described in verses 2–16 consists of phony desires generated by an *ersatz* culture. Now he knows better and wants only "to be near God" (v. 28).

It occurs to me that Sabbath is a school for our desires, an exposé and critique of the false desires that focus on idolatry and greed that have immense power for us. When we do not pause for Sabbath, these false desires take power over us. But Sabbath is the chance for self-embrace of our true identity.

I finish with a pause at verse 23:

> Nevertheless I am continually with you;
> you hold my right hand.

I recently heard a Lutheran pastor describe a woman who had walked seven hundred miles as a refugee to escape a violent war and was finally able to cross a national boundary out of the war zone. She walked all that way and brought with her an eight-year-old girl, who walked beside her. For seven hundred miles the child held her hand tightly. When they reached the safety, the girl loosened her grip, and the woman looked at her hand. It was raw and bloody with an open wound, because the little girl had held on tightly in her fearfulness. It is like that in verse 23.

> Nevertheless I am continually with you;
>   You hold my right hand.

This is no casual hand-holding. This is a life-or-death grip that does not let go.

"No-Sabbath" existence imagines getting through on our own, surrounded by commodities to accumulate and before which to bow down. But a commodity cannot hold one's hand. Only late does the psalmist come to know otherwise. Only late may we also come to know. We may come to know, but likely not without Sabbath, a rest rooted in God's own restfulness and extended to our neighbors who must also rest. We, with our hurts, fears, and exhaustion, are left restless until then.

STUDY GUIDE

THE FOLLOWING STUDY GUIDE, WRITTEN BY MARTHA Bettis-Gee, is meant for individual or group study. Please adapt it for your needs. Each chapter has an opening prayer, a number of questions to consider, an activity to practice if you are reading this over a six-week period, and a closing prayer written by Walter Brueggemann.

Session 1

PREFACE and SABBATH AND THE FIRST COMMANDMENT

Opening

Open with the following prayer:

Holy One of Israel, in a culture characterized by restless anxiety, we are indeed weary and heavy laden. Teach us about Sabbath rest. Give us a new understanding of how that gift can free us from our commodity-driven existence into life of neighborly relationship. In the name of the One who calls us to take his yoke upon us, wherein we can find rest, Jesus Christ. Amen.

Exploring

Discuss, or reflect on, some of the following:

– In the preface, Brueggemann reflects on his memories of Sabbath when he was growing up, characterizing Sunday as a time when "Thou Shalt Nots" prevailed.

• What do you remember about how Sunday was observed in your family when you were a child?

• What activities, if any, were prohibited in your household?

• If you grew up at a time when blue laws were in effect, how did that affect how your family observed the Sabbath?

– The author observes that Judaism can reeducate Christians concerning our own faith and practice, pointing us to the work of Michael Fishbane on the maintenance of Jewish mindfulness in a culture that is increasingly more mindless.

• How does he distinguish what he calls our "Adamic" selves from our "Mosaic" selves?

• What does Brueggemann suggest about Fishbane's use of the term "divestment"?

– Brueggemann cites Patrick Miller's observation that the fourth commandment on Sabbath is the "crucial bridge" that connects the Ten Commandments together. Why?

• In what way is the Sabbath commandment drawn into the exodus narrative?

– The author observes that the first commandment is a declaration that the God of the exodus

is unlike all the gods the slaves have known—
a God committed to covenantal relationships
rather than endless production.

• What is implicit in the reality of God's willingness to engage in Sabbath rest?

– Brueggemann contends that ancient Egypt's
socioeconomic system must be understood to
understand our God.

• What parallels do you see between that system and our own socioeconomic system?

• Would you say we live in a system where people
are commodities to be dispatched for endless
production or where they are subjects situated
in an economy of neighborliness? Why?

– The author notes that God's restfulness, in contrast with restlessness, characterizes God, ensuring
that restfulness is at the center of life. He points
to "either/or" choices continually placed before
ancient Israel and evident in the teaching of Jesus.

• How does he characterize these stark choices?
How would you?

– The author invites us to ponder the "other gods"
of market ideology and the systems they authorize in our contemporary context, offering a
number of examples that call up endless desires
and needs that can never be satiated.

• What are some of the messages these systems
communicate?

- • What are some of the consequences of a commitment to these gods?

- – YHWH issued a call to "let my people go" to release the Israelites from Pharaoh's system of endless production.

  - • How is Sabbath a practical act of resistance and trust?

Responding

Commit to the following practice for the coming week:

- – What are some ways you can keep the Sabbath so that Sabbath-keeping is less anxiety driven? Make a list of the activities in which you and your family normally engage on a Sunday. Include activities at your church, including worship services, meetings, educational programs, and youth group activities. Also list other routine activities, such as grocery shopping, cleaning, yard work, soccer games, or other athletic activities in which your children are involved, and list media activities such as viewing sports events or other programming, social media, and Internet surfing. Underline those activities that you can identify as characterized by Sabbath restfulness. Now circle those that you can identify as anxiety-inducing. Show your list to family members or a close friend; or if you are doing this study in a group, show it to another participant. Commit to eliminate as many activities that do not provide Sabbath restfulness as possible, or at least to reduce the time you spend doing them.

– In the coming week, pray the following prayer as a part of your time of devotions. Identify for yourself what holds you in bondage. Reflect on where you experience the flash of God's emancipation. Give thanks for the God of Freedom.

Closing

Pray the following prayer:

Loving Back the Emancipator *by Walter Brueggemann*
(On reading Exodus 20:1–6)

The demanding, relentless brick quotas
  kept arriving at daybreak for our ancient mothers and
    fathers.
They faced the harshness of harassment;
  the heat of the kilns,
    the bristles of straw collected.
And then, abruptly, all of that ended . . .
  because you, Lord of liberty and justice, in an instant on
    a dark night,
  you led our mothers and fathers out of bondage in sing-
    ing, in dancing, and in joy.
We remember that ancient bondage. We recall the flash of
  your emancipation.

We know that bondage now among us:
  bondage of our caves of self-preoccupied, insular living,
  bondage of our tribes of the like-minded in fear of all
    others;
  bondage of the market and our mad chase after more;
    bondage of theater where we live make-believe lives.

But we ourselves also know the flash of your emancipation.
>   And because of that flash,
> we know who you are;
> we know the future you would give us;
> we know your passion for justice;
> we know your deep love for us and for our world.

And so we love you back, wholly, without compromise or
>   distraction,
> with all our heart, all our mind, and all our soul.
We will not so passionately love any other,
> because you are the source of our life and our future.
We give you praise for your ancient deliverances.
We give you thanks for your liberating presence with us now.
We give you honor and glory for you good future to which
>   you summon us.
You are the one who makes us "free at last." And we love
>   you! Amen.

Session 2

RESISTANCE
TO ANXIETY

Exodus 20:12–17

Opening

Open with the following prayer:

> God of the covenant, we come before you carrying
> the weight of anxieties we often find difficult to cast
> aside. In a world of many competing priorities that
> leave us restless and unsatisfied, we yearn for Sabbath
> rest. Blow the freeing winds of your Spirit on us. Help
> us resist the gods of our culture. In the name of Jesus
> we pray. Amen.

Review last session's practice:

Revisit the list of Sabbath activities you listed from the
last chapter and the one anxiety-inducing activity you

chose to eliminate. How fully did you live up to your commitment? Think about or discuss the following:

- Did I choose to eliminate an activity that affected only me, or did the activity also affect family members? If family members were involved, how fully did they opt into my action?
- How did eliminating this activity impact my Sabbath rest?

Exploring

Discuss, or reflect on, some of the following:

- Brueggemann observes that our understanding of Sabbath has become enmeshed in life-denying practices that contradict the intentions of Sabbath and misrepresent Sabbath-keeping.

  - How does he define Sabbath when taken seriously by faithful Jews and Christians?

- He characterizes ancient Israel's arrival at Mt. Sinai as an occasion to enact "regime change" and to acknowledge the rule of the covenant God.

  - To what does Israel's oath primarily pertain?
  - What stark contrasts can you identify between the relationships called for in the Ten Commandments and what the regime of Pharaoh represented?

- Brueggemann observes that Pharaoh was an

endlessly anxious presence. Name some of the
sources of that anxiety as detailed in the chapter.
- He notes that God spoke ten times in fire and
smoke. How did God's claim of exclusiveness as
delineated in the first three commandments dif-
fer from the exclusive claims of Pharaoh?
- We read that a deep question was posed for those
who had just been liberated from slavery in Egypt:
How does one regard the neighbor seriously when
one has imbibed the profound anxiety of the
Egyptian system? We might ask that question in
our own context: How does one regard the neighbor seriously when one has imbibed the profound
anxiety of a consumer/commodity-driven system?

• How do you respond?
• How does the author suggest God counters
anxious productivity?

- How is the faithful practice of work stoppage—
for our neighbors as well as for ourselves—an act
of resistance?
- Consider the practical implications involved in
ensuring the faithful practice of work stoppage
for our neighbors:

• In an increasingly interfaith culture, what
does it mean to ensure work stoppage for
those whose Sabbath falls on a different day
of the week?
• How do we affirm work stoppage for those
for whom Sunday is a work day—our pastors,
church educators, and other church employees?

- How do we support work stoppage for those on the margins—persons who must work two or even three part-time jobs in order to put food on the table for their families?

Responding

Commit to the following practices for the coming week:

- Brueggemann tells us that ceasing work allows our anxiety to wane, and he invites us to counter anxious production with committed neighborliness. He affirms that faithful practice of Sabbath is an act of resistance. Revisit the list of activities in which you are involved on the Sabbath.
- Identify which ones not only are anxiety-producing for you personally but also have implications for the neighbor.
- Identify one such activity over which you have control that you might eliminate—for example, doing your grocery shopping on Sunday.
- If you are in a group study, discuss with others activities you might be able to impact together. For example, is your church heavily programmed on Sunday? If so, do all the church's programs enhance Sabbath-keeping, or do they inhibit it?
- Again use the closing prayer in your devotions in the coming week.

    • Pray the first portion of the prayer. Then in silence, reflect on those situations and conditions about which you are fearful, acknowledging them and lifting them up before God.

- Pray the second portion of the prayer, giving thanks for the creating, sustaining God. Ask for God's guidance in seeking to be more peaceable.

Closing

Pray the following prayer:

Falling Back into Reliable Goodness *by Walter Brueggemann (On reading Exodus 20:8-11)*

From the outset you called the world, "very good"!
Unlike you, we find the world a dangerous, demanding locus
        for our lives:
    We are beset by fears of scarcity and running out.
    We are visited by fears of falling behind and not measuring
        up.
    We are occupied with rumors of war, danger, and terror.
    We are frantic to protect our little places of well-being.
    We are weary of achieving and accomplishing.
    We are exhausted with neighbors who seem to us like com-
        petitors and threats.
In our anxiety we find the world at best bearable, but less than
        "very good."

You, creator of heaven and earth!!
    You are so unlike us!
You do the orderly proper business of creation, of
    seedtime and harvest,
    cold and heat,
    summer and winter,
    day and night.

You sustain the regularity of seasons, sun, moon, stars, and
  wind.
And then you pause in confidence.
 sure that the world will hold,
  unworried about scarcity,
   certain about flourishing,
    unbothered about the threat of chaos.
We imagine you peaceable, cherishing your good world, at
  leisure,
 not restless, anxious, or worried.

We are so unlike you in our anxiety and fatigue.
We resolve, nevertheless, in your presence,
 to be more like you,
 to imitate you,
 to fall back into quiet confidence and serenity.
Like you, we may trust that your world will hold.
Like you, we may enjoy the good order of your creation.
Like you, we may be at rest and unanxious.
We are so unlike you; and you are so unlike us.
And now, in this moment of honesty before you,
 we promise to replicate your restfulness,
  finding ourselves able to bask in your reliable goodness,
   unanxious, unafraid, unbothered, unworried,
    defined by your durable goodness. Amen.

Session 3

RESISTANCE
TO COERCION

Deuteronomy 5:12–14

Opening

Open with the following prayer:

> Gracious God, too often we ignore your gracious, redemptive action in our lives. We forget to remember that we need not be enslaved by anxiety and loss of confidence. We forget our deep connection neighbors. Forgive us, O God. We'll try harder. In the name of Jesus we pray. Amen.

Review last session's practice:

Revisit the anxiety-producing activities you identified that also have implications for the neighbor. Consider the activity over which you have control that you committed to eliminate from your Sabbath.

– What impact did eliminating that activity, or shifting it to another day, have on how you experienced Sabbath rest?

– What neighborly impact did this have? If choosing to refrain from this activity on the Sabbath had no direct impact on whether others were able to experience a cessation of work, what influence might it have had on family members or friends and how they view Sabbath-keeping?

Exploring

Discuss, or reflect on, some of the following:

– The author describes what happened when the ancient Israelites acted out of their acute anxiety and created a god out of their most treasured commodity, gold. Though the Holy One nullified the covenant, Exodus 34 describes how YHWH was willing to begin again, offering new commandments to articulate the restored covenant.

   • What was distinctive about how the Sabbath commandment was stated?

   • What are the implications of exercising dominion over the earth?

– Moses gives instructions to the people concerning the promised land they are about to enter, with the goal of ensuring that the people understand that the covenant of the desert still applies to the fertile lands.

- • Why does Moses consider the land of Canaan a temptation and a seduction?
- • What is meant by Brueggemann's statement that prosperity breeds amnesia?

- – We read that being in the land poses a conflict between two economic systems.

  - • How are these systems described?
  - • How does each system frame what it means to live properly?
  - • Which one holds the danger of generating an economy that is anti-neighborly?

- – If, as Brueggemann asserts, the covenant is immediately contemporary for each new generation, then what are the implications for the context in which we now live?

  - • What yardstick do we use to measure how we meet the challenges of environmental degradation?
  - • What yardstick do we use to measure the increasing gap between the haves and have-nots? Of what it means to make decisions based on the common good?

- – Following 9/11, people of the United States were challenged to be better consumers, better shoppers in order to respond to the attacks. In the Sabbath commandment as articulated in Deuteronomy 5, the phrase "that they may rest like you" challenges the gradations of performance, worth, and significance of the consumer culture and interrupts the coercion of producing and consuming more and more. Respond to Brueggmann's list of things that we are no longer coerced into doing.

– Which of those items on the list of coercion hold the most power over your life?

• What other coercive expectations could you add?

– In Deuteronomy the motivation for Sabbath is not creation but remembering the exodus and the coercive competition of quotas. Reflect on the questions the author asks:

• Do you fall asleep counting bricks?
• Do you dream of more bricks you have to make yet or of bricks you have made that are flawed?
• What are the bricks that disturb your rest?
• What do the words "Remember the Sabbath Day to keep it holy" mean to you?

– Moses imagines the Sabbath as a new social reality. People who keep Sabbath live all seven days differently.

• What two aspects of new life does the author highlight that could be made possible by breaking free from patterns of coercion?
• What is radical about these aspects, and how do they address the vulnerable ones in our society?

Responding

Commit to the following practices for the coming week:

-   We read that Sabbath is not just the pause that refreshes. It is the pause that transforms. Consider what it would mean if we "seven" all our days. Reflect in the coming week on how you might live all seven days differently. Jot down responses to the following in the coming week.

    •   How would your day-to-day routine be transformed?
    •   With Sabbath-keeping as your framework, what activities, priorities, and attitudes might you leave behind? What might you add to your routine?

-   As you pray the closing prayer in the coming days:

    •   Locate yourself within the old grind of master and slave, in the hopeless, graceless contest of greed. Imagine yourself on the way from master-slave to neighbor.
    •   Pray for strength for the journey and for the courage to embrace neighborliness.

Closing

Pray the following prayer:

Now as Neighbors by Walter Brueggemann
(On reading Deuteronomy 5:12–14)

We remember the old harsh days of master and slave;
    some were ruthless, demanding, unforgiving,
    others (most of us!) were fated to urgent performance.
But then you vetoed those presumed arrangements
    when we walked through the waters of freedom
    and we found ourselves with no commandment but to love
        neighbor.
We know now, in our own experience, that it takes a neigh-
        borhood to make a life.
We could not, however, sustain that alternative for very long.
We fell back to old patterns.
    Some of us became slaves again:
        some ended in hopeless debt;
        some bondaged to addictions that came to define us;
        some frozen in deathly emotions;
        some enlisted into the rat race that we cannot win.
Some of us, by luck or by hustle or by blessing, became masters:
    we made money and could leverage others;
    we gained property and with it clout;
    we earned pedigrees and came out on top;
    we got credentials that entitle us to more;
    we outmatched our fellows and came to command them.
Without notice, we have returned to the old grind of master
        and slave,
    brick quotas and
      hostility and
        exploitation and
          alienation.
It all happened without notice;
    we find ourselves recruited in a hopeless, graceless contest
        of greed.
You, however, call us back to neighbor.
    You put in front of us our hired help, the worker class, the
        service industry, immigrants, the hopeless poor.

They are so unlike us who manage and administer and
control.
Except that in your emancipatory presence, they are so like us,
entitled to rest,
assigned to dignity,
assured of viability,
intended for security.
They are like us, permitted rest and leisure, respect and well-
being.
We are on the way from master-slave to neighbor.
It is not an easy way, and we go there reluctantly.
But we go there because of you.
You are our first Good Neighbor.
And you intend us all to be good neighbors,
not on top of the heap to feather our nest (or nest egg),
not at the bottom of the pile to grovel in despair.
But neighbor, bondaged only to mercy, compassion, justice,
and generosity.
Give us courage to be on this journey together. Amen.

Session 4

RESISTANCE TO EXCLUSIVISM

Isaiah 56:3–8

Opening

Open with the following prayer:

> God of the globe, and indeed of the whole cosmos,
> help us to move beyond the fences we erect to see the
> expansiveness of your gracious call. Guide us as we
> look beyond the boundaries that block us from those
> we may label as "others." And as our vision expands,
> nudge us to consider uncomfortable truths and to take
> risky actions. In the name of Jesus we pray. Amen.

Review last session's practice:

If you are engaged in this study with a group, reflect
with a partner on the statement from the previous chapter that Sabbath is the pause that not only refreshes but

111

also transforms. Discuss with your partner your understanding of what it would mean if we "seven" all our days. Talk together about your experience in the past week of seeking to live all seven days differently, with Sabbath-keeping as a frame. Or reflect by yourself on the following:

- Name any activities, priorities, and attitudes, however small, that you were able to leave behind, as well as anything you added to your routine.
- What was the most difficult aspect of the changes you made? Where were you tempted to give in to old patterns? How likely are you to be able to continue to resist coercion?

Exploring

Discuss, or reflect on, some of the following:

If in a group study, discuss the process by which Israel was transformed from "no people"—a marginalized, objectionable people—to "this people"—an identifiable, intentional community. If you are studying the book on your own, review the process for yourself. What risks were involved in such a transformation?

- We are introduced to two great interpretive traditions of Torah: the Priestly tradition and Deuteronomy.

    • How did each define ancient Israel's membership—who was in and who was out?
    • What elements in the text give us clues as to

the serious nature of membership and how urgent the elimination of risk?

– The author point us to Isaiah 56, a later text that again returns to the issue of membership, of critical concern for a people who had returned from the Babylonian exile.

• What groups, previously excluded, are now included?
• How is the requirement of keeping Torah spelled out?
• How does Sabbath deconstruct the notion of being qualified for membership?

– The author spells out the consequences of our current state of fearfulness: our efforts to fence the world in order to keep others out.

• Where do you see evidence of the desire to build fences—or walls—in our culture?
• Over what issues is the church currently embroiled in an effort to identify who belongs and who does not?
• How do you respond to the proverb that good fences make good neighbors?

– Brueggemann reflects on what counts: our fruits, the outcomes of our lives, not our pedigrees. Reflect on the Scripture passages that distinguish good fruits from bad fruits. He observes; "I dare to think that 'good fruits' arise from the 'peaceableness' of Sabbath." How do you respond?

Responding

Commit to the following practices for the coming week:

- In the coming week, use the spiritual practice of examen to examine the good fruit and the bad fruit of your day-to-day life.

  • Light a candle and settle into stillness, breathing in and out deeply and becoming aware of God's presence.
  • Silently read Galatians 5:19–21. Then ask yourself the following: Where in my actions or attitudes did I give evidence of the bad fruit of which Paul is speaking? Where do those bad fruits arise from rat-race living? Bring those actions or attitudes before God, asking God's forgiveness.
  • Silently read Galatians 5:22–24. Ask yourself the following: Where in my actions or attitudes did I give evidence of the good fruits to which Paul refers? Offer those actions or attitudes to God in thanksgiving. Ask for the will to embrace those good fruits and for further discernment about peaceableness of Sabbath.
  • End with a time of silence.

- Reflect on the author's observation that Sabbath is a refusal of the grapes of wrath and an embrace of the good fruits.
- Pray the closing prayer in the coming week. On concluding, reflect in silence. Ask yourself:

- Perhaps I am feeling smug because I would include all those whom Brueggemann identifies as "others." If so, who are "others" to me? Conservatives? Liberals? The wealthy? Those whose worship is too stuffy, too shallow, too intellectual? The uneducated or biased?

- Pray the prayer again, asking forgiveness for the sin of exclusion and reimagining what "all of us gathered together" might mean.

Closing

Pray the following:

All of Us Gathered Together in Sabbath by *Walter Brueggemann*
(On reading Isaiah 56:3–8)

It seems right and good to be God's chosen people.
   We enjoyed friendship with God;
   we were assured special blessings from God;
   best of all we got the land of promise as our very own.
But then, immediately, other peoples began to crowd in on us.
   First it was the Canaanites and the Philistines;
   then it was the "yellow threat" from Asia;
   later it was all the intruders from south of the border.
     and now we have to contend with too many Blacks,
     and many insistent Native Americans who will not go
      away.
     And now it is Muslims!
It has turned out that all these "others" are now with us;
   they crowd us and disturb us and compete with us.
Of necessity we devised rules to protect our specialness;
   we formulated laws of purity

and made a list of all those things that disqualified others.
  We made rules for race and ethnicity and gender and
      pedigree;
  we made it all safe and secure from all alarms.
And then, right then, abruptly, you uttered your shattering
      word:
  It is for "all peoples" . . . "my house a house of prayer!"
We blinked, we wondered, we debated:
  Did you say "all peoples?"
    All peoples like foreigners?
    All peoples like eunuchs?
    All peoples like Mexicans?
    All peoples like Muslims?
We checked the text; we interrogated the ancient poet.
We investigated your own ancient history of xenophobia.
  And the word was confirmed: you did say "all peoples"!
In that utterance you undid our sense of specialness;
  you undermined our purity laws
  and our best self-serving formulations.
We looked and discovered, as we had not seen,
  the sweep and wonder of your governance,
  the largeness of your vision,
  and the expansiveness of your house of prayer.
We looked and then noticed, as for the first time,
 that the company of those who trust you is very large,
very mixed, very diverse.
We watched, and saw that you are gathering others alongside us.
  You have gathered us as your chosen,
  but your gathering does not stop with us;
    you gather others as your people.
All of us, those who have long been chosen,
  and others now gathered,
  all of us at prayer in your house;
  all of us at Sabbath in your creation;
  all of us together in covenant;
  all of us together, according to your wide purpose. Amen.

RESISTANCE
TO MULTITASKING

Amos 8:4–8

Opening

Open with the following prayer:

We come to worship longing to encounter you, O God. Yet often our attention is scattered, our minds on other things. And sometimes we are fully attending, but not to your presence: rather our minds and hearts are occupied with other gods—the cultural gods of commodity. Call us to account. Give us the strength of will to resist. Turn us to you and away from commodity. Help us to worship in spirit and in truth. Amen.

Review last week's practices:

Review with a partner, or reflect by yourself, on what you discerned as a result of practicing the examen in the past week. Call to mind what good and bad fruits emerged in your times of discernment over the course of the week.

- For what did you ask God's forgiveness? For what did you give thanks?
- Consider what it means to be "in": Is it having the right pedigree, or is it demonstrating the fruits of the Spirit? How would you define inclusiveness?

Exploring

Discuss, or reflect on, some of the following:

- Brueggemann points us to the prophetic tradition for a critique of ancient Israel's compromised and inadequate ways of keeping Sabbath.

  - How does he define "the turn to commodity"?
  - Who in ancient Israel's history does he identify as a representative embodiment of commodity restlessness?
  - In our context, what individuals or groups can you identify who also exemplify the same kind of commodity restlessness, with its threefold acquisitiveness?

- Read the three prophetic references the author cites that expose the fraudulent nature of a distorted Sabbath (Isa. 1:12–17; Hos. 2:8–13; Isa. 58:1–7). Discuss, if you are in a group study, or reflect by yourself on the following: What do we learn about faithful worship and Sabbath-keeping from each of these prophetic utterances? What indication does each prophetic utterance give that Israel's worship is phony or inauthentic? The author now points us to the prophet Amos and what the author calls a fuller, more direct oracle. To get the full impact of this oracle, read it aloud to yourself (or to the group).

– Brueggemann notes that the exploiters engage in false worship even as they are watching the clock, eager to return to distorted, dishonest trade. He calls this practice out and identifies it as the epitome of multitasking.

   • What examples does he cite?
   • What other examples can you give?
   • When have you been guilty of multitasking in the midst of worship?

– Correct or faithful worship, we are told, is worship that leads to justice for all, especially the most vulnerable.

   • What elements would need to be present for worship to lead to justice?
   • What connections can you make between this kind of worship and authentic Sabbath-keeping?

– Consider some of the prevailing practices in churches as congregations strive to be relevant to those they seek to attract: projection screens, sophisticated media, polished contemporary music, and the like.

- What are the positives of a market-driven approach to evangelism and ministry?
- What do you see as the downsides?
- Is it possible to use the language and approaches of the marketplace without also "selling out" to marketplace values?

Responding

Commit to the following practices for the coming week:

- Brueggemann defines multitasking as "the drive to be more than we are, to control more than we do, to extend our power and effectiveness." Common sense indicates that if one is trying to do two tasks simultaneously, one or the other will suffer, and the body of research bears this out: doing more than one task at a time, especially more than one complex task, takes a toll on productivity, despite what many people think.

  - Resolve in the coming week to consciously resist multitasking. Identify the areas where you are attempting to serve two masters to the detriment of one. For example, if family members are texting at the dinner table, commit to turning off cell phones for the duration.
  - On your own or with a partner, engage in a sacred reading of Matthew 6:24, using a practice known as *lectio divina*:

- Read the verse slowly to yourself. Note what word or phrase stands out to you.

• Read the verse again, **meditating** on what God may be saying to you.

• Read the verse again, then **pray**, answering the question, what do I want to say to God?

• Read the verse again, **contemplating** what you want to do, based on your prayer.

• As you pray the closing prayer in the coming week, reflect on the following: What does it mean to take time to be holy?

Closing

Pray the following:

The Costliness of a Rushed Sabbath *by Walter Brueggemann (On reading Amos 8:4–8)*

We have been summoned forever to listen
  since the first "Shema" of Moses [Deut. 6:4].
We were not sure whom the poet addressed;
  but then he specified:
    you who trample,
    you who ruin the poor,
    you who eagerly rush to exploitative business or exploit-
      ative sports,
    you who rig the scales,
      and cheat the poor with weights,
      and leverage interest rates,
      and manipulate tax laws,
      and wage theft when we can.

We did not think it pertained to us, we good people,
    because we did not notice, we did look carefully,
    we did not recognize our own participation,
    we do think systemically about how our benefit is enmeshed
        in such subtle violence.
But the poet knows:
    the poet saw that the poor are had cheap;
    the poet laid out how we treat the poor in cheap ways,
      how we push chaff as grain,
      how we cut corners with the vulnerable,
        creating food deserts
        and failed schools
        and flawed services all around.
The poet did not quibble; he saw and spoke the raw hard
        truth.
He saw that we wanted no Sabbath from profit;
      no rest from exploitation,
      no break from self-fulfillment at the expense of others,
      no slack in shopping or entertainment or indulgence.
He saw that our self-celebration vetoed the old command of
        Sabbath, because
    we could not wait,
    we could not pause,
    we could not put off success and growth and wealth and
        domination.
In response,
    the poet offers us words from God who is not mocked,
    from the Holy One who sees through our fake piety.
What words they are!
    The creator of heaven and earth notices our wee self-
        serving maneuvers;
    the Lord of history takes note and will not forget as the
        evidence piles up.
And the outcome of our unacknowledged shenanigans
        returned to us by the holy God? The news is not
        good even if given in terrifying poetic imagery:
    The land trembles in destabilization; who knew?
    A big sadness comes among us; who anticipated?
    A force of chaos like a rising tide; who was ready?

Flood waters of disorder; who could tread that much water?
We could call it an act of God,
   or an environmental crisis,
   or a loss of safety:
      A world order under threat?
      A violent society?
      A failed economy?
      A lethal ecology?
All because we have rushed through Sabbath; we could not
      wait.
We could not take time to be holy,
      because holiness, amid the rough and tumble of the real
         world,
      will not get us a cup of coffee. Amen.

Session 6

SABBATH AND
THE TENTH COMMANDMENT

Exodus 20:17

Opening

Open with the following prayer:

> God of the ages, our present age is shaped by our inces-
> sant drive to have more stuff. The gods of commerce
> and power seduce us into believing we are defined by
> the quantity of our possessions not by the quality of
> our relationships. Quiet our endless, restless search for
> stuff. Bring us into the quiet center wherein your Spirit's
> call is clear. In the name of Jesus Christ we pray. Amen.

Review last session's practice:

Review with a partner, or reflect by yourself, on the
commitment you made to avoid multitasking in what-
ever situation you chose.

- What challenges did you encounter as you sought to focus your attention on relationship rather than tasking?
- What did you learn about yourself? What master are you serving?

Exploring

Discuss, or reflect on, some of the following:

- Brueggemann observes that the commandments on neighborliness reach a climactic point in the tenth commandment on coveting.

  • Why does he see coveting as the ultimate act of destruction of the neighborhood?

  • What does he identify as a mistaken interpretation of the commandment's meaning?

  • What is the meaning of Sabbath rest in the context of this commandment, and how does it relate to love of neighbor?

- He explicates the meaning of coveting, pointing to two aspects of this community-destroying greed:

  • To what do "house and wife" and "slaves, ox, and donkey" refer?

  • What is the significance of the repetition of the word "neighbor"?

- Brueggemann describes the recurring practice in the ancient world of pitting agrarian peasants against urban elites, an inherently uneven and coercive contest.

- What is its contemporary analogue?
- Can you cite specific examples where the vulnerable are at the mercy of the entrenched economic forces?

– Some would say an understanding that the common good must serve as a curb to unbridled economic forces is an outmoded idea.

- Would you agree? Why or why not?
- What evidence can you give that this idea is or is not a driving force today?

– Brueggemann cites several biblical texts that exposit the tenth commandment. In a group study, group members can choose to read one of the texts; or on your own, read one or more of the texts and the author's commentary. Discuss, or reflect on, the following:

- In each of the Scripture passages, what points to the understanding that coveting is the active capacity to seize what one wants, not just the desiring?
- What clues do we get to the eventual consequences of coveting, whether of land or of other possessions? What happens when the rights of the vulnerable are ignored?

– The author also gives us five instances in the teachings of the early church that illustrate the importance of the implications of the tenth commandment. On your own, or in the group, what can you say about the significance of each of the following contrasts: thanksgiving/acquisitiveness; old self/new self; craving/gift?

– In the culmination of the study, Brueggemann returns to the assertion that in the commandment on the Sabbath, commandments one and ten come together: both idolatry and greed are rejected because they reduce living to commodity.

  • What does he mean when he suggests that Sabbath is a big no to idolatry and greed, but also more than that?
  • Why is Sabbath a school for our desires?

Responding

Reflect on the following for the long term:

– The author reminds us of the first line of the old hymn "Take Time to Be Holy." He suggests that perhaps it would better read, "take time to be human," or even better "take time." Finally, he observes that "Sabbath is taking time . . . time to be holy, time to be human."

  • Revisit the ways you were invited to respond over the course of the study. In what ways was your understanding of Sabbath transformed by seeking to resist the culture of now?
  • What long-term changes can you embrace in order to take time: time to be holy, time to be human?

- In the coming weeks, return to the prayer that closes this session. Make these words a part of your continuing meditation as you move forward to "seven" your life: "We pledge in your presence, greater resolve for Sabbath"

Closing

Pray the following:

On Choosing Neighbors *by Walter Brueggemann*
(On reading Exodus 20:17)

Our master rabbi told a tale of building bigger barns, to store more grain to have more stuff, because the man did not have enough yet. Before he told the tale, he said simply, "Be on guard against all coveteousness" [Luke 12:14]. Or we translate "greed":

"Be on your guard against all kinds of greed; for one's life does not consist in the abundance of possessions."

When Jesus said that, he appealed back to Moses at Sinai. Via Moses at Sinai we received ten lordly words. The second word was about the worship of things: "No graven images" [Exod. 20:4–6]. The tenth is: Do not covet;

Do not be greedy.
Do not be acquisitive;
Do not accumulate;
Do not hunger and thirst for more.
The Lord of Sinai has set limits:
Do not covet your neighbor's house;
Do not covet your neighbor's wife;
Do not covet what belongs to your neighbor.
Do not covet . . . and then three times,
neighbor,
neighbor,
neighbor.

We live, each of us and all of us,
in an economy of coveting:
The tax and mortgage laws are designed to let the powerful accumulate more;
The ads are designed to make us desire what we do not
need;
The out-of-control military is designed to protect unsustainable
advantage of things in the world;
The ecological threat is the result of cravings that violate
the limit of sustainable creation.
The tax laws, the TV ads, the strong military, the ruin of creation,
all serve to impinge harmfully upon the neighborhood.
The tax and mortgage laws prey upon vulnerable neighbors.
The ads seduce us to value things as substitutes for relationships;
The military ideology turns neighbors into enemies;
The exploitation of the earth refuses to reckon with rab-
bits and radishes as neighbors.

But we have known better since Sinai!
We know, when we do Sabbath pause, that we can live well
without an updated computer or phone;
without another new car;
without elective cosmetic surgery;
without remedial drugs, etc., etc., etc.
We cannot and have no deep desire to live without neighbors.
We confess our anxiety about scarcity,
about not yet having enough and being left behind.
We confess, when we do sabbath pause,
that we do not treasure neighbor enough,
the one close at hand;
the one far away;
the one who shows mercy;
the one who needs mercy.
We pledge in your presence, greater resolve for Sabbath,
that we may submit our restless anxiety to your alternative
future,

that we may refocus our lives in your gracious will;
that we may trade coveted things for treasured neighbors,
that we may come to our true selves, liberated from the
    tyranny for more.
At sundown on Sabbath, we will gladly and loudly declare,
    "Free at last!" Amen.

CPSIA information can be obtained
at www.ICGtesting.com
Printed in the USA
LVHW011054201118
597735LV00001B/74/P